Bards Annual 2016

The Annual Publication of The Bards Initiative

Bards Initiative

James P. Wagner (Ishwa)—Editor, Compiler

Nick Hale—Submissions Editor, Compiler

Marc Rosen—Associate Editor

J R Turek—Associate Editor

Cover Art: Vincent (VinVulpis) Brancato

Layout Design: James P. Wagner (Ishwa)

Editing and technical assistance

Judy Turek

msjevus@optonline.net

Bards Initiative Staff

President
James P. Wagner (Ishwa)

Vice President
Nick Hale

Treasurer
Marc Rosen

Council
Jillian Roath
Lorraine Conlin
Ed Stever
Sharon Anderson
Margarette Wahl
J R Turek
Aaron Griffin

Foreword

In your hand you hold the 6th edition of Bards Annual. So much has happened in 6 years. I remember being proud of gathering 39 poets together for the Examination Anthology back in 2010 (the predecessor to Bards Annual) and now, demand to get into the anthology has gone up and up with each year; as a result we've not only had to be more and more selective of whose work we include, but we've had to restrict acceptances to 1 poem per poet. Even so, Bards Annual 2016 with over 140 poets is the most populated edition to date—and every poet truly earned their way in.

No one can say that Long Island poetry is anything but thriving and growing. We're seeing more and more events with 50, 70, or 100 people in attendance. Our bard's family has extended this last year and grown in more ways than we could have ever hoped or dreamed.

In October 2015, roughly 3 months after our 5th anniversary of Bards Day on Long Island, we saw the launch of the first ever NoVA Bards Anthology (Northern Virginia), poetry headed up by our vice president Nick Hale who has formed a poetry group down there. (A meetup group now consists of over 400 members and growing.) The event that launched the NoVA Bards Anthology was small compared to our typical Bards Day up here, but a big time poetry event for what they were used to down there. So many of the poets who participated were happy for the chance to share their work with other people— many having considered poetry a personal hobby since they were in school and didn't have many avenues for its expression.

For the last 3 years the Bards here on Long Island have held an event called "Bards Against Hunger"—the event raises food for a local pantry and we plan on continuing this tradition. But what was unique about this last year's Bards Against Hunger is that down in Northern Virginia our companion group hosted a similar event in their area—this gave us the idea that perhaps we could spread the Bards Against Hunger poetic tradition to other places in the country—each focusing on a food shelter local to them, to let the mainstream community see the good that poetry can do.

As for our local scene, each year we add more poets to the table. And sadly we lose a few as well—one notable loss this year was the one and only Maxwell Wheat; founding father of our community, one who has taught and inspired so many who the community will surely miss. But we can take pride in knowing that he got to experience the golden age of poetry that Long Island has been seeing, and we know how much he would love to see and greet the new faces that are entering the poetry community of Long Island day after day.

The Long Island poetry community is sometimes unaware of how unique and well organized we really are when compared to other poetry communities throughout the country. In fact, now that Bards has expanded, we've seen just how much other poetry communities can learn from modeling specific events and books after the way we do things here on Long Island.

Congrats on another year dear bards, 6 years running, stronger than ever before, and many more years to come! Let's appreciate the treasure that we have here and keep sharing and expanding. And most of all, keep writing!

~ James P. Wagner (Ishwa)
President, Bards Initiative

Table of Contents

Introduction

During the early days of the Bards Initiative, fellow co-founder, James P. Wagner, and I wrote and spoke a lot about our philosophy of poetry. We would often assert that poetry is the "voice of the people." We wrote about poetry's power to unite people, to give voice to the disenfranchised, and to bring about positive social change.

We were not wrong. In the years since we founded the Bards Initiative, we have seen poets come together to show solidarity with and raise aid for those suffering in the wake of global tragedies. We've seen poetry unite very disparate groups of people and sit at the root of many very unlikely friendships. We have also seen poetry, time and again, serve as a means of expression for those whose voices would have otherwise gone unheard.

The Bards Initiative has come a long way since then. We've seen many people come and go, both in our organization and in the community. We've watched shy young poets grow into experienced, savvy writers and performers. We've seen the wonderful diffusion of styles as primarily page poets write with more consideration for performance and primarily performance poets give more consideration to how one would read their writing. We have certainly exceeded the expectations we had for our little organization.

Through the years and the countless events, our philosophy of poetry has remained unchanged. As our community of poets has grown, we've begun networking with other like-minded communities across the country, including my poetry group in Northern Virginia. Through these new connections and friendships, we can achieve more than we ever thought possible years ago. We can bring together *communities*. This will allow us to amplify the good that we do through our various projects and events, share ideas, styles and philosophies with a wider range of people, and give the poets in each community a wider range of exposure, something that many poetry communities I have been a part of have somewhat lacked.

During a round-robin reading I attended in Fairfax, VA in late 2015, one poet in attendance forgot to bring material with him to read. Before the reading, he was thumbing through a copy of *Bards Annual 2015* I had with me. Each time it was his turn to read, he chose a poem from the volume that stood out to him. Sometimes he would introduce the poem by reading the poet's bio first or explaining why he selected it. It was an excellent experience. This sharing of ideas and poetry can only help to make our communities better as we bring more great poetry to Long Island, and bring more great Long Island poetry to other places.

Regardless of where you may be from or living now, I hope you enjoy these poems, however they found you, as you delve into the latest volume of the series that started it all.

~ Nick Hale
Vice President, Bards Initiative

Lloyd Abrams

an already lost child

she sits on the park-green
paint-peeled bench
with her fifteen-year-old face
or maybe she's nineteen
with eyes looking as vacant
as the child's
who's perched on her knee
their only interaction
the contact
between threadbare jeans
and diapered bottom
while her boyfriend
or man friend
it's so hard to say
is hunched over
in his khaki green puff jacket
smoking a cigarette
sipping out of a paper-bagged can
absorbed in whatever is displayed
on his cracked cell phone screen

they're sitting together
sitting apart
bringing an already lost child
into an unforgiving world

Esther Alian

In Pursuit Of...

Happiness
Elusive
A myth?
Attainable at the bottom of a glass, then a bottle, then two
Which man has found you?
Kept you?
Can any divulge your presence
Or do you flit by swiftly
So that we only recognize your likeness
Once you have left our midst
Or do you have another face
A two-headed serpent
Joy intertwined with unbounded sadness
All soaring heights anchored by the irons of loss, memory,
disappointment.
Wherefore do you reside?
Within our soul?
Without, in a wider universe to be explored and traversed?
Within others, gatekeepers to our peace?
I think, all of these
And yet
Your company tirelessly I seek.

Donald E. Allen

Meteor Shower

Our memories are stardust
made of moments in our lifetime.
As we live, these gather and shine like the stars in the night sky.
An endless abyss,
filled with bright spots that scintillate
every time a person comes into view in our mind's eye.

Then like shooting stars,
even the smallest memory blazes in a moment of brilliance
as one of these people we knew, these memory makers, passes on,
and an empty space in the night sky of our memory is left behind.

When **many** friends pass...
over a short ticking of life's clock...
it is like a meteor shower,
that leaves the night sky of our lives... a bit dimmer.

We can recall the light that used to be
in that spot ~now gone dark
but the twinkling,
and our memories,
fade over time.

With the passing of others

a little bit of ourselves passes as well.

And so...
As we get older
we must continue to fill our lives,
with new stars,
new glittering memories,
friends that shine,
moments that sparkle...
or someday
our night sky
will go dark.

Sharon Anderson

Unfettered

Poetry brooks no rules,
respects no boundaries.
It goes where it wishes,
does as it pleases.
It shatters illusions, or
conversely, creates them.

Poetry transcends time and space,
mounts an army of ideas,
then slays them
with one stunning phrase.

It speeds down highways,
wanders barefoot
through silent forests,
dives fearlessly into oceans,
chases joyfully after random butterflies,
stumbles, weeping, into caverns of despair.

Poetry challenges our frailty,
lauds our strength,
plays jester for our merriment,
cries eulogies for our sorrow.

Poetry, like our universe,
is always expanding,
revealing new stars,
opening our eyes and minds
to new explorations.

Poetry brooks no rules,
respects no boundaries.
It goes where it wishes,
does as it pleases...

demands that we do the same.

Peter Arebalo

I Used To Live Here

A child scribbles visions of things yet to come
flame flickers filling chambers
shifting light along the constructs of a world made manifest
Compacted molecular potentials erect an embodied template
A temple uncoiled from a seed
That temple tempered to a cage
There's so much more to say
There always will be

A self, created to brace against all parts unknown
A reflection
Etching flesh with opinion
Stuck to guns
in celebration of shallow waters
How would you explain to someone
that you
talking beast
are more than a man
more than sweat and flesh
a blossom sprung from a pearl
petals red, tips drenched in living gold

Who am I to talk like that?
When ledgers and houses need work

Schools, roads and practical obligations
Pave over identity
"real" value lies in service rendered
Our pound of flesh asks
that we grow invisible
transactional
conversational
It's heart shattering to bloom in a world of such percussive value
When
you an unfolding flower
This small piece of earth
An expression
that blessed this place with its appearance
A life of such essence
Like forcing a drop of water to be everything it's ever
brushed against
The silt, the humidity, the tundra, your cheek
Each place devoid of permanence
Its property without definition
As long as it quenches thirst

Frances Avnet

I Want My World Back

I don't want to have to think that:
the tourist next to me has a bomb in his suitcase,
the commuter leaning against the pole is going to slash my face,
I'll witness my favorite donut shop being robbed.
I want to
Walk on a college campus and not hear bullets,
Sit at a café in the City of Lights and not worry about bloodshed,
Eat in my kitchen and not have to duck bullets.
I'm tired of seeing armed soldiers at the train station and airport
and wonder if they are protecting or suppressing us.

Bob Baker

Watching What I Eat

I went to a buffet,
And I watched what I ate;
As I ate and ate and ate,
Lots of food, plate after plate.

Now many people say,
If you are trying to lose weight;
You are not going to lose any,
Eating non-stop at that rate.

And I say you are so wrong,
As wrong as can possibly be;
If you want to understand,
You just have to listen to me.

Lots and lots of food,
On my plate did appear;
And I kept on eating,
So it did disappear.

So the plates were getting lighter,
Of this there can be no debate;
So that is proof positive,
I must be losing weight
With each passing plate.

Julie Baldock

Onomatopoeia

I read a quote by a famous woman
who writes shows starring famous women–
complicated women–
about the glass ceiling:
"Think of them. Heads up, eyes on the target.
Running.
Full speed.
Gravity be damned...
Running,
Full speed
and crashing.
Crashing into it and falling back.
Woman after woman...
How many women had to hit that glass
before the first crack appeared?"
When I read that,
it makes me wanna slam my body into walls;
makes me want to shoulder check
the next person who steps into my space–
who makes himself too familiar–
who thinks he knows something about me
by the things I say when I talk–
the way I move when I walk
by the fact that if he wanted to refer to me
I'm a she.

So maybe there are things that I can't be.

My friend texts me from babysitting
middle school girls–
there must be a better word for that,
they aren't babies;
my friend texts me from being paid
to sit with young ladies who are actively living through the
darkest period of their development–
we'll work on that title–
and asks me how I can stand it
to watch my son struggle with friendships and crushes–
the unbearable highs and lows of adolescence.
She describes their secret, coded behavior
and all the rules that must be observed to make it through the day.

I'm surprised she needs the reminder:
it's different for girls.

See, they make onesies for baby girls
That say "I hate my thighs"
And they hang them up next to the
"Superman" one for boys
How could you hate a thing like that?
Fat, little rolls of soft perfection
And I want to whisper in the ear of every baby made to wear it:
One day, girl, you're gonna stand on those legs
And walk away from all the places and people
Who told you you couldn't be super because you weren't a man.
I'm sorry they told you that.

I'm sorrier if you believed it.
But, damn if the deck wasn't stacked against you the
First time someone thought making you feel less than
Was a commoditized joke.

And I think of those women–
the ones running towards the glass–
How when the light hits just right
They can see their reflections
and they are fearless
They know that the odds have never been in their favor
and they are most likely going to fail-
there are some clubs invite-only but their names are off that list,
there are doors they will never find the keys for
and years will be wasted looking at rings overstuffed and jangling,
weighted down and always somehow just the wrong shape
but today,
they are warriors
and they are brave
and they are running,
reaching out their hands like salvation
as they link arms to make a wall to hit the ceiling
knowing that there have always only been two possible exits-
things either bend or they break–
but today the thing will not be them
as they shut their eyes
and they hold their breath
and they listen for the crack that sounds like change.

Sybil Bank

Husband

Sometimes he has a slight shamble to his walk.
When did the road the endless flow of ongoing shining
become dusty like an elephant's skin?

When waves lifted you like weightless light,
ascending mountains of rush, foam and spray
hurling you to the glistening strand,
you shook off water like a satisfied seal
after a lip-smacking fat fish catch.

Now the sea, daunting in its high tide wakening,
rushes to your knees, throws you grappling the undertow,
drunken seaweed snakes, and crackling bits of stony shell.

A letter returned after a tired journey, the bedraggled envelope
black-stamped: *Address unknown,* like the dark bruise
after your cataract surgery when they brought you back to me.
Our dark puffy winter coats waiting to be taken home.

And here you are my kind, excited man, alive and well.
Relieved that after anesthetic, you know exactly
where and who you are.

And who I am.

Patricia Z Beach

The Red Thread to China

Adopted children and their parents
Are connected by a long red thread
It reaches to their hearts and brings them together
No matter the distance, the times or weather
This thread reached to pull us across and bring you home
Destiny was set when we met our beautiful baby in Hefei
It made you the lovely young woman you are today
Across centuries and continents
We've always known each other
Now I am the one you call Mother

Antonio Bellia (Madly Loved)

Caveat

As words of
Equality and freedom
Are loudly spoken,
False ideologies
Discriminate against
The free human soul,
Against the freedom
To achieve
The liberty to
Succeed.

Sedated with promises
Of false security
We sell our
Human inheritance
For an effortlessly gained
Bowl of soup.

As a rabbit in a
Cage
Will no longer remember how to
Dig a warren,
As a salmon in an
Aquarium

Will not know
To swim upstream,
As a wolf on a
Leash
Will forget how
To hunt game,

So you, human, with
All your innate gifts,
All your precious talents,
With your creative wealth,

You could become stunted,
Crushed within
The vise grip,
Addicted to sugar treats,
Scorbutic
In a society afflicted
With mental rickets.

Don Billings

Thoughts at the Checkout

Do you see her there … the girl with amazing hair?
See how it flows in strands of rippling gold ~ ~ ~
Down over her shoulders in unconcern.
It seems she has a serious way about her,
Standing there tall and slim.
And sometimes, just for an instant,
She lifts her head slightly … off somewhere
And the faintest of smiles
Gives a moment's revelation of her inner being.
Little does she know, my thoughts at this moment.
Little do I know …
What thought has made her smile.
So I tell her: *You have amazing hair …*
And now, I no longer remember her reply,
Only her fleeting smile and the golden flowing strands.

Maggie Bloomfield

Another Season

Another season fades, leaving
serpentine vines, spiced residues.

Uneaten fruits crumble damply
in shadows, unmattering back

from an island
of summer.

A now
molders underfoot.

In black subterranean caves
roots and sealed seeds
flow toward fall.

Time's measure flares
boisterous, chafes -

like us,
longing to stay.

Peter Bové

The Clams of Summer

I miss diggin clams outta the sand
And jumpin thru waves over my hands
Feel the icy waters chill
Run thru me like a carnival ride thrill

Then to lay naked in the sun
Reliving all the fun

Soon it gets too hot
To beg the ocean not
So once again I go
To let cold waters flow

To deepest reaches in
Until they reach the sun
Oh the fun!
The fun!
The fun!
To ride the Oceans run
The dangers disappear
And sometimes so the land

But sideways then we go
Till the waves take us home
Ahoy! Ahoy! Ahoy!
Let us eat some clams

Richard Bronson

The Rams of St. Kilda

We're driving down the road,
two lanes merging, and on my right,
a black Cadillac SUV –
he coming up fast from behind.
Suddenly, we're in a race.

I hit the gas and we each
lunge forward.
My *Volvo* takes the lead,
his *Caddie* left behind –
tailgating, puffing, fuming.

My wife gives me a look –
why do you care? "I know," I say,
"a woman wouldn't get involved,"
and I think of the rams of St. Kilda,
who go into rut once a year.

Their gonads swell as autumn approaches,
switched on with the shortening day.
Then driven by testosterone,
they charge each other –
head butting head
until one remains, king of the herd,
the others stumbling away.

Alice Byrne

Attachment Theory

With sudden and incendiary speed the electricity arcs between us.
With us, it's always been that way.
A flash of light across some distant sky,
A clap of faraway thunder, coming closer.
A stallion rears to jump the corral to reach the heated mare.

Nothing need be said, although we have.
Lips that have felt the famine of apartness
Now are quenched by my waiting mouth.
I am open and agape.
Now he loves me. Now he hates me. That is how great the power.

I feel good, full and loved.
Bang all of a sudden he zooms into power drive.
Fire drive.
Yet another gear we couldn't have dreamed was there.

The world fades, gone.
Silent stars with their silvery moons.
One hundred billion galaxies lay before me.
Afloat in timelessness lit with explosions.
The Enterprise explores heretofore unknown worlds.

His body curls around me. He is ferocious.
An angry tiger protecting his mate.
He tries to swallow me and I am consumed.

Paula Camacho

Fickle Fashion

The colors this year are black and gray
The fashion expert said
I must run out to buy new clothes
My closet is full of red

The fashion expert lured me on
I sat there mesmerized
But carefully eyed my wallet
When she said *accessorize*

Needing jewelry for our new boots
Made her savvy pitch clear to me
That cost should never deter us
From a shopping spree

Your face, my dear, must look alive
Forget the muted hues
Heavy red lipstick is back again
Along with clown eyed blues

Stiletto heels must be worn
Regardless of the pain
They reflect a certain fashion sense
Not that you've gone insane

I look forlorn at all my clothes
I am a fashion don't
Unless I buy the newest things
There is very little hope

But wait, what did she say
About the next new style
I quickly grab up the dress
I dropped on the discard pile

For next season we will see
She replied with a flick of her head
That the bright new color trend
Will be everything in red

Anne Coen

High School Reunion

We were taught
    to solve for x and bisect angles
    analyze Shakespeare
    write thematic essays
    place an order for steak and fries in several different languages.

We understood the laws of physics:
    how opposites attract and sometimes repel.
We put each other under the microscope
    and learned to become suspicious, rebellious.

I wonder if I need
    to forgive you
    for the slights suffered,
    both real and imagined
    rumors as rampant as food fights
    notes intercepted in class
    items stolen from lockers
except that I no longer recall
what we fought so vehemently about.
I distinctly remember forgetting that.

None of this matters now.
We are all students of life
learning the curriculum of the heart
verse by verse.

Joseph Coen

Bard's Light

On an overcast, damp day
in a wood paneled room
at a historic place
a bright light pierces the darkness
as friendly faces gather
to speak words into the dark day

Strong words, true words
weave stories, paint pictures, bare emotions
No race, no color, no social class
all are one
in the ardent desire to tear the grey net surrounding us

The clear light of poetry
and the warmth of friendship
envelop and shine forth from all
and transform the place

Arleen Ruth Cohen

Stuck

They told me to push.
I pushed until I
felt my guts would bust.

My face darkened.
My cheeks bulged.
My eyes watered.

They told me to push
but nothing moved.
The pain from my
efforts almost unbearable.

Finally the car rolled
out of the muddy hole
the tires making
a sucking sound.

Latisha Coleman

This is for you
Yes you
The same one who doubts herself
Underestimates your worth
And occasionally thinks about cutting yourself
Somehow death seems to be on your mind a lot
The thought of being able to die and be born again just to see
if anyone would miss you
This is for you
The same one who fails to see their worth
Being so caught up worrying about everyone else
And their thoughts
Somehow the energy is drain is focusing on the wrong things
This is for you
The same one who gets overwhelmed being there for
everyone else
But hates the fact that the same gestures won't be returned
back to you
It gets under your skin how your kindness is taken for weakness
by so many
And it's nerve wrecking how you're taken advantage of
This is for you
The same one that loves and hates love at the same time
Because every time
It was the same results all the time
You want to give up on love

But you find yourself still craving the touch of love
Love
It's bittersweet
With the credentials to cut you deep
But yet can be so sweet when it wants to be
This is for you
The same one who's around so many
But still feels all alone
The disconnection from yourself and the ones around you
Affects you so heavily
But I want to be the one who tells you
The world needs you
Your mission is your mission
And no one else's
Life will attempt to distract you
Attack you, forsake you and confuse you
But we all face it
The question is, can you take life head on strong with a cause and
correct its wrongs?
Do you have the courage to still be who God wants you to be?
I believe you do
I believe in you
I know you believe in you too
This is for you.

Chris Collins

Seeds Of Hope

I've only been given a few credits in life, one being a good soul
But what is it worth having when one's life is not whole;
The beaten, the battered and abused parts
Mindless is the mind when you are tearing at the heart
The strings being plucked like the guitar being played
Every note matters just like words on a page;
So we are stricken down fighting against our own fears
The worrisome and sick shredding in tears
Cause part by part, day by day death is calling
It's the life we choose to live the worst can be enthralling;
So I am silly, I am shy, but want to explode up in the stars
To open me up and look past the flesh and scars
For I am to be one, part in this planet like the seed that starts
the growth of trees
Once as a child, I now grow slowly to the man I hope to be

Lorraine Conlin

Radio Days

Dad loved junking
He'd find radios tossed on the dumps
repaired some, dismantled others
invented a purpose for useless parts

He'd wrap wire wave-transmitters,
around bits of twigs or Popsicle sticks
straighten coils and springs
made many misshapen spools

Mom used his so-called junk on
nights he worked or was away
She'd free hand draw the
petals, stamens and leaves
on folded crepe-paper
cut, shape them between her thumbs
curl the tips with an old butter knife
wire the faux foliage to stems

She taught me how
to make paper roses
bend wire back and forth
feel the cold metal get hot
just before it breaks

wrap petals onto metal scraps
by twirling strips of tape

I cut my thumb and forefinger
on razor sharp radio wire
till I learned to work the spools

He'd say, *Never Waste,*
She'd say, *Finish Whatever You Begin*

Jane Connelly

Mosquito University

I HAD mentioned this before…
Stop being so bourgeois
So middle-of-the-road
Stop dripping the color beige
Try wearing tangerine, magenta, cerise
Perhaps, at once, with a splash of lime?
That night the Perseid showers were raining down
Across the timeless sky
By the beach, near the reeds, and
I wore my beekeeper's hat
Much to your dismay and consternation
As we watched the constellations
Your eyes rolled, with your nostrils flaring.
I thought I'd never hear the end of it
Until mosquitoes shied away
From me, to dine on you
Who came, so beige and bourgeois, but
Left so red, and blue.

Lisa Corfman

Cast In The Soul

To life is
Eighteen.
Double chai,
36 is life in thee.

At that age, parents are many,
But youth is still there,
Children are running,
Wait, don't go in there.

At that age I am now,
In a slump all alone,
But hoping, just hoping,
For friends in my home.

Moving forward is life,
And life takes its time.
I just want to be,
To be grateful with a happening life.

Home is the place,
That rests in the heart,
And age is the thing,
That home will not stop.

When one finds the age,
that is true to the heart,
Healing occurs,
But time cannot stop.

Whether home or away,
18, 36 or 72,
The lord's ceramics are memories,
Cast with love in the soul.

Steven Couzzo

A Blind Eye

What do you see when looking into a blind person's eyes?
Their thoughts, their feelings, or maybe their need to still be.
Life without sight leaves one to change their whole lives.
To still want to live and love, work and play, as when they
could see.
Or maybe their world was one that they always had been
without sight.
That all that they know has always been that way,
and never known the loss.
To not know day from night, or to have only known the warmth
of the light.
To only know things in your own way, and to learn what you
may at all costs.
To live without sight cannot be imagined, only experienced
through the blind.
Taking the time to mingle and befriend, and share a little of
yourself is wise.
You may get to know yourself better, and be glad of what
you may find.
Only in this way will you get to know, what you see in a
blind person's eyes!

Alexandra Curatolo

Mom Wanted

I need a mom with eyes as blue
      as the beautiful sparkling sky above us.

I want a mom who **understands** my words
      even when I don't.

However, I need a mom who *guides* me
      through my life but doesn't take over.

I need a mom who trusts me in the kitchen
      even after all of my mistakes.

I want a mom whose hair has been kissed
      by bright, *golden* sun.

Though, I need a mom who will keep teaching me
      about music (especially **ROCK&ROLL**)
         as long as I shall live.

I need a mom who has enough love
      to give both my sister and me.

I want a mom whose skin is the color of
      a *beautiful* plain untouched

by any human being.

But I need a mom who will make me laugh,
     even when I'm not sad.

I need a mom who delicately places a Band-Aid
     on each of my problems.

I want a mom that gives me courage
     when I need it most.

However, I need a mom who **teaches** me
     valuable life lessons that I will always treasure.

My mom is every one of these things and more,
     and my mom would know which writing piece
          is **mine** for sure.

Jeanne D'Brant

Many Waters

Did it start with the St. Lawrence?
Gentle waters lapping hard ridges under submerged toes
No, it was Lake Champlain and home waters
gathering clams in metal baskets, found with unafraid feet

Of course it was the boat at the beginning
racing across the Great South Bay
Captain Father at the wheel, Mother with her black hair blowing
standing in queendom in the bow

Came the Dead Sea and the Red Sea
which did not part for me
Heading wide-eyed to the Qa'aba in Holy Muslim Mecca
Chanting "Allah hu Akbar!"

Aegean mornings, waking on the sand
Velvet evenings bathed in ouzo and starlight
Diving into crystal deeps, down, down
to pick starfish off the bottom of the sea

The tiny Azores, pin point volcanic tips
in the mighty maelstrom of the Atlantic
Just a fuel stop before heading across the Sahara
Dazzling dunes rolling like the waves of a sandy sea

The Tyber and the Arno and the Po
The cobalt Mediterranean lapping on the shores of stony Sicily
Sicilia, where the sirocco smells of Africa
Ah, Africa, the wind like a furnace of fragrant flora and spice

The mighty three-headed Volta races to the equator
amid heated banks on red sandstone shores
Ashanti memories, talking drums on riverbanks
nights of passion locked in the lovers' embrace

Cross the cold grey Kattegat which feeds the Baltic Sea
stalked in all seasons by the menace of sea jellies
Umbelliferous eyes bobbing below in a boreal sea
Icy winds bear me to the stone cold city of the North

The tepid Thames snakes self-importantly
under the Tower of London that eats royal heads
The Seine curves sensuously in the sinful city
where the rose light of Notre Dame sweetly seeps

Steaming up the broad and moody Elbe
returning to my Black Forest lover
We holed up in Hugo's flat in Rotterdam,
rolling joints by a winter wild North Sea

The Rhone and the Rhine, the Danube and the Don
The Shannon estuaries where river rams the open ocean
Did I first sight you from a long boat with a dragon on its prow?
My DNA dances in remembrance

Hail Caernarvon Bay and the waters of Snowdonia
Twisting airily under blasted slate mountains
which stand blue grey in the thick Welsh mists
near to Camelot and magical Merlin's cave

The Vispa boils in Zermatt, glacial milk
a silver stream in the shadow of the Matterhorn
Where haute skiers in designer shades
make their ascent in Kardashian fashion

The land-locked Caspian, home to Homo erectus
The cold springs of Paumanok's lake, Ronkonkoma
Slow brown rivers of Belize, teeming with crocodiles
Whose open maws pant the Kundalini Breath of Fire

The Jordan and the Karun River near Isfahan
The Helmand above Qandahar, shiny, stagnant, green
It was there I knew my destiny
belonged to Zeus and Zoroaster

Countdown, waters swirling
Blue planet whirling
Let me have more of you
before my dance is done

Caterina de Chirico

A Hundred Hours

When we meet in the summer of our years we are each other's best company, sitting on the edge dangling our feet chanting *Gâté Gâté Parasam Gâté* hail the goer!

And the goer goes beyond the beyond until she knows what she came here for, until she doesn't need hands to feel, lips to kiss, or legs to mingle in union,
until he doesn't need eyes to see, ears to hear or a tongue to taste communion.

A hundred hours of ecstasy our spirits are finally free to soar, where we can stop

famine crime and war and farther still to where we cannot count the time
and the doors are all open with nowhere to go.

A hundred hours of ecstasy and there's nothing to gain, nothing to choose, nothing to cling to and nothing to lose.

A hundred hours of ecstasy, and it doesn't matter if we stay or if we go only that we came.

Douglas Dennison

Petals

The stalk must be snapped at its base
as soon as some blossoms decline.
The cluster of pinwheeling reds,
dispensed with, to wilt on the ground.
A pair will appear and supplant
each stalk that is cropped with its blooms.
You taught me that this is the way
to make a geranium thrive.

The flowers that deepen their hue
and curl at the edge must be plucked.
Umbrellas of color collapse
to shrivel and brown in the beds
Receptacles, nuded, renew
with buds that will shortly unfurl.
You taught me that this is the way
to make a petunia thrive.

My garden that summer was crowned
with annuals braiding the sun.
But blossoms when dropped to the dirt
surpassed those that stayed on the plants.
I left them because the discards
continued to offer their hues.
Like Caesar you plundered my yard,
as petals were strewn at your feet.

Linda Trott Dickman

The Fishing Boats

*For the fishermen and first responders from Rockaway Beach
Oregon and the sea they serve.*

ONE
Shakes her many tiers,
castanets in furious accompaniment
her sandy dance across the floor.
Menacing layers limn haloed crown.

When her lover responds, his pleasure
swells to great heights.
This is barely time,
but when his jealousy peaks
he chases her from far away
and she
just keeps dancing
long shallows.

TWO
Waves galloping
manes blowing like sea spray.

Lightning like Sauron's blink.
Thunder, howitzer punctuation
rising above the roar, the howl.

Foam bunnies scurry across the shoreline,
For what is man that you are mind-ful of him.

Cloud formations dissolved into waves,
like Clydesdales, they pounded my spirit.

THREE
The Light from a single fishing boat
dividing star from surf.

Then, like fireflies
five flickered in the cold.

Like living sparks coming up for air
growing, glowing at the promised catch,

Lucifer foiled in doing his work,
holds them in winter's chill only.
And then there were eight.

FOUR
Goodbye moon,
Goodbye logs that would choke a *balrog,*
    the slough of a tsunami.
Goodbye legions of sea foam steeds.

This dancer has seen,
she leaves with sandy slippers,
tied with heartstrings to this violent coast.

Sharon Dockweiler

Mustard

I hate mustard.
It always makes me cry.

It's not like onions.
There's nothing chemical about it.
I just don't like the taste.
No. That's not true.
There's more to it than that.

Knowing my aversion,
My father used to aim the mustard at my hot dogs,
Smiling as if offering a treat.
Rescuing my plate, I ran from the table in tears.

It soon became my chore to fill the mustard bottle.
Knife scraping deep into the jar to pour it into the squeeze bottle,
The yellow goo got all over my fingers
Which I automatically licked clean.
Dad stood by and laughed.

Boyfriends, too, found it funny
That I didn't like the stuff.
They snuck it into peanut butter sandwiches,
Squeezed it in my tea.

The day I cleared my father's things out of the house
I realized.
No longer would I need to keep the mustard in the fridge.

I tossed it in the trash.

Likewise, as each cruel suitor walked out of my life,
The mustard jar was banished with him,

Until now.

On this fine day,
Ambling slowly in the park,
Pushing your wheelchair down the hard-packed path,
We celebrate one of your last *good* days
With hot dogs from a vendor.

I bend to kiss the mustard from your lips.

I love mustard.
But it always makes me cry.

Peter V. Dugan

Algorithm Of Self

A split second lingers
    a big bang ensues.
Protons, neutrons and electrons
    fuse and fizzle
as atoms and molecules
    form
    new elements
        of perception.

Inner space and outer space
    open
to explore a universe
        of awareness.
Dimensions collapse
    time and space
        without constraints.
Colors heard, sounds seen.
    black and white
fade to gray
    then change
into a cacophony of color.

Musical notes float
    and

dance like leaves
    on the wind.
The physical and spiritual
    unify.
Barriers of separation,
    recede.
An illusion caused by the delusion
    of perception.

The search for meaning
    devolves
    into
a scream,
    a whimper,
no form, no reason
    only distraction.

I wash down dewdrops
    of sanity
        with red
        homemade wine.

Circle the black hole of my soul,
    the heart
        of darkness.

Forget social niceties
    and
    request
        the go code.

Vivian Eyre

Inside My Raincoat

The lining. Middle seam shreds
along the hard ridges of my backbone,
how to care label separates from its binding.
I walk out the door
into sharp strips of streetlight.
The cold city scissors my back,
the fretwork.
Every move widening seams
around my eyes. Why should I leave you—
when everybody has its' patchwork,
hard lines and little hurts that fray?

Heart lines so different than a line of trees,
that predictable hug contours of city streets.

Who's to say how long a trench coat
remains a shield from rain,
or whether life lasts in the lining,

to enfold the body in warm embrace,
above jagged edges of shadow.

Elizabeth Fonseca

Facing Ordinary

Reaching neither greatness nor lies,
day by day she scours the limits
of her life, its dailiness, and she in it,
working, fixing rice, meetings, reading,
too much occasional wine, watching as
(almost without knowing) in the scouring
the limits of her self are outlined, her character:
where it cramps or fades; worse maybe,
where the line is indelible, fat
and black and precise,
where the harbored dreams scuttle away
sideways
like crabs, the harbored dreams are
swiped away like cobwebs, and she
at the line of her life: "Ordinary,"
it says, and she, facing ordinary,
courts moon ray, words, and the rain.

Kate Fox

The Magic of Music

Your sweet face
Melts my heart
Overwhelmed by the
Memory of your voice
I would give anything
To hear you speak

Wondering how to
Get through to you
I turn the music up
Unaware this is the
Key to the door
That will bring you
Back to me

We Will Rock You
Moves through the house
Pulling you into it
Giving you words
Carrying your voice
Outside of you and
Into the world

Meeting you

Once again
I am reminded of
The Magic of Music

Shilpi Goenka

The Blank Screen

I wonder often,
As I sit in contemplation,
Filled up to brim with desires,
And stare at the blank screen.
I wonder, perhaps, the screen
Is staring at me too,
With a similarity of emotions,
Which are unseen yet exist,
Beyond my imaginings,
And earthly understandings.
And, as I start to press each key
Of the keyboard, the letters on the keyboard
Come to life on this screen, each one
Breathing so intensely, panting perhaps,
On the white screen, not blank, anymore.
And, I wonder, the blank screen still
Stares at me, for more, thirsts for more
Letters to satiate its longings,
Prods me, provokes me, and pierces me.
And I have no choice,
The waters stir uncontrollably
Tonight, and like a ritual,
I offer what all I contain

In the secret chambers of my heart
To this blank screen.
The fingers help to ease the process.
And, to bring some relief,
I sip from this chai tea latte
Which only exacerbates the pain,
Of the memories linked to it,
The brief moment sealed upon
The screen timelessly...

Jessica Goody

Bitter Tea

The tea was bitter with betrayal.
Their knowing eyes met across the table,
among the sugar tongs and strawberries.
Blackflies lingered over the sugar cubes,
waved away by impatient hands.

The spoons rang against the teacups with
a chime like church bells. The ice clatters,
catching light like glaciers in a sepia sea,
melting fast under the steady eye of the sun.
The rising steam unfurls to meet the sky,

evaporating like a jet's contrail overhead,
its warm scent drifting against perfumes.
Smiling over sandwiches, Mrs. stirs angrily,
Her jaw strained taut with furious hostility.
The teasing frisson of electricity leapt

between their mingled fingertips. Concealed
beneath the tablecloth, She tickled his ankles
with her painted toes, her sandals abandoned
in the grass. A cool green afternoon awash with
light, drifting tendrils of windblown hair and

laughter like wind chimes, bone china gleaming
against her vermillion fingertips. The strawberries
bleed against the porcelain. The world is green and
expectant. The leaves shiver in the breeze, throwing
shadows on stippled bark. The fresh-peach scent of

the bower sweet as the summer nectar of sweat-damp
sheets, a strand of hair stark against the pristine pillow.
Her legs are crossed decorously beneath the whiteness
of the napkin stained with the blown kiss of her lipstick.
The sunlight illuminates her shape through the voile

of her summer dress like stained glass, lit from within.
He lingers in the curve of her neck, kissing its white
softness and murmuring in her ear. They whisper into
the wind, stealing secret moments of breathless
conversation, fingerpainting their linked initials on the

sweating glasses and smearing them clean. The civility
of convention, the pouring of the steaming pot, leaves
unfurling. The crystal click of ice cubes clattering in
the topaz tea, sugar swirling like sand, the sharpness
of citrus filling the air. The long spoons catch the light,

winking at their duplicity. Mrs. worries the teabag with
a spoon, watching the water darken. The broken shards
of their relationship cannot be repaired with decorum
and cups of tea, pallid weapons against the calculating
sensuality of Her smile, as ripe and overt as summer fruit.

Aaron Griffin

Umber

Arriving in City Hall Park via the Brooklyn Bridge one May morning, I came across a squirrel.

His coat was ragged and worn with age, but the burnt umber that set him apart from every gray Manhattan squirrel in the park drew my attention to him, and he noticed me, and my Belgian waffle topped with berries and cream.

He was serious, following me, right at my side like he belonged there, until I found a quiet bench to enjoy my breakfast.

And the squirrel was there, sitting on the bench, less than an arm's length away, as he inched closer still, with a hopeful look in his little black eyes, which met mine with such deliberate focus.

He tried to take a seat on my lap.

"Don't mess with me. I know you're a transformed human playing cute to get food and stuff. Go panhandle elsewhere." I said calmly, allowing myself the pleasure of a bit of fantasy in that moment.

Hopping off the bench, the squirrel went from person to person, making eye contact with each human and seeing how far that got him.

He locked eyes with a woman standing on a bench taking photographs, with an infant in a carriage, and so on, attaching to and following each, until at last he accumulated a crowd, snapping photos and tossing scraps of food.

He played to the crowd too, making cute poses, letting people pet him, anything for attention, and food. I'd never seen any squirrel, let alone a Manhattan one, act like this in my life.

In my head, I named him "Umber," and throwing my waffle carton away, I moved on.

Back in that same park, a month later, as the East River shimmered with the golden light of the setting sun, I returned, searching for my squirrel.

There were many gray squirrels around, but the aged master manipulator who's fur was the color of autumn leaves was nowhere to be seen among the paved pathways and grassy greens where I had first seen him that time he tried to beg my waffle away.

But there was another squirrel, and for whatever reason I began to follow her instead, at a calm walking pace.

City squirrels are of course accustomed to people being nearby, but knowing I was tailing her, she walked away from me, as I continued to follow, past benches where people watching must have wondered what I was up to.

I'd followed her all the way to the edge of the park, where the paved path opened toward the entrance to the Brooklyn Bridge walkway, the limit of her domain.

She doubled back, down the path, and I followed, to her obvious distress.

Maybe realizing I wouldn't stop stalking her, she stopped at the foot of a tree, and turned to look at me.

That look she shot me, after having been shadowed nearly half a block down through the park, transmitted so clearly her annoyance.

With my mind filling in the blanks, the squirrel might as well have said, *"Alright human, what do you want?"*

And engaging in the fantasy of being able to telepathically speak with animals, I responded,

"I'm looking for your friend. The old squirrel with the dark brown coat who's extra friendly toward humans."

And from somewhere within my brain, perhaps the part which provides dialog to be spoken by characters encountered within dreams, merged this response:

"You're too late to see him down here. He makes his rounds courting people for food only in the morning. At this time of day you'll find him napping up in the trees. Now stop following me."

And with the idea of these words having just barely solidified in my mind she scurried up a tree, and vanished into the green canopy.

Imagining that the gray squirrel had really spoken to me, I headed back into the park.

I was still actually searching for the umber flirt of a squirrel after all, and where else could I look apart from the ground than up above, but what were the odds that out of all the trees in this park and all the squirrels living here that I could possibly look up the first tree I see to find –

Umber. Laying quiet and still, spread across a sturdy tree limb, in just the right spot to catch a warm ray of afternoon sun that had pried its way through the parasol of leaves.

He was high up, but just close enough to the ground for me to see that it was him, his deep autumn coat shimmering in the sunshine as he dozed, with me the only human in the park having noticed he was there.

Pleased with myself, I left the park and walked over the Bridge, seeking further magic.

Concetta Guido

Woodstock Rap Escapade

The times are distorted,
Tossed around,
Longing for Doo Wop ways of
"The Hop" and "The Twist."

And instead we're graced with
The evolution of
Garbled rap, twerking, jerking,
And peak.

Unable to comprehend
Cryptic autotune and singular
Repetitive lyrics of
One night stands
Drenched in the veils of
A frothy night club serenade.

Where did meaningful stories go?
Where lyrics beheld simplistic tales,
Poodle skirts and saddle shoes,
Motown and their unification of harmonized song.

Peaceful flow of Woodstock
Chanting of love and peace.

Dancing like the children of freedom
Just don't care
In an array of flowers and caked in mud.

Today we chant sex and drug discreet,
Lacking harmonious sways;
Replaced with thirsty longing
For thumping club speakers
And gyrating to a beat no one will remember
When the morning comes.

Maureen Hadzik-Spisak

The Leaning Tree

We have come a long way
This leaning tree and me
Despite its curve
It umbrellas its spindly limbs
Spreads its broken joints
Shielding the house it shades
I have cut away the undergrowth
So I can lean against its curve
Its skin is flecked with knots
I feel its sap pounding in my fingers
Or perhaps it is my own pulse
In autumn its leaves will fall
But for now they are curled
Refusing to give up their mystery of life
And so we bend together
This leaning tree and me

Nick Hale

Poem Snake

The Snake slithered through me
the other day
and he asked, with haste
"Can you feel it?"
I said, "Yes, it fills me!"

I felt nothing at all.

And the Snake, he said
"Do you see that?"
and I, with closed eye,
"I can see it, proud and clear!"

And the Snake said
 "Now son, we have a job for you."

I said "You're not my dad!
Don't tell me what to do."
And he was stunned,
for a syllable, then
tried to interrupt,
hisspered trust in my ear.
I trusted him instead.

Snake said, "We know that you've been down, son,
and we know what you can do.
For the cash that you have on ye-
we'll make a deal with you!"

Inexplicably intrigued, I told him to go on.
He promised me endless riches,
power
on a cosmic scale.
He promised immortality
and the things I've never had.
"Once you're one of us,"
Snake said, "you will become a god."

So, against my every judgment,
much to my surprise,
I forked out my life savings,
and the snake said "Close your eyes."
Warm softness closed around me,
pushed me into somewhere wet.
Still waiting for my power.
I haven't felt it yet.

Let me tell you a story
of how you can change your circumstance
for the low price of all you're worth
paid out in advance.

Sylvia Harnick

Monarch

monarch butterflies soar free
glide on currents land pristine
some keep flapping
arrive with tattered wings

fly thousands of miles survive
to procreate live for six months
bask in the sun hang loose
display their colors

when our nest empties we recover
find equilibrium on wings of others
happiness by light of day
live freely know
contentment within

Robert Michael Hayes

Poppa

He came all the way across the Atlantic
from the great Isle of Potatoes.
He landed at Ellis Island
and found refuge in Queens.

From Sunday to Saturday he labored,
no longer on his farm
instead in the dark tunnels of the subway.

But, each eve he tirelessly toiled
in a small dirt patch,
tending his beloved vines,
surrounded by concrete,
growing sweet, succulent tomatoes.

George Held

A Bellport woman named Madeline Vetch
Had a husband who was surely a wretch,
So she served him an aspic
And laced it with arsenic,
And she wound up in Sing Sing for a stretch.

Gladys Henderson

Film Clip

Dedicated to those who jumped on 9/11

He steps off
into the bright light
as if a dancer
in perfect form,
left leg slightly bent,
right foot pointing
towards the earth.
He wears a perfectly
pressed suit, and
a white shirt gleaming.
With arms outstretched
he begins to whirl,
a Shinto prayer
wheel spinning,
spinning, descending
between the towers.
His body reflects
on the glass windows
as he falls.
He is always there,
in mid air, when
I think of him,

never reaches
the ground;
he is spinning,
whirling, each
turn a prayer,
a prayer.

Judith Lee Herbert

Songbird

Her words are leaving her,
like birds flying south,
silhouettes across the moon.

In conversation at a family dinner,
I joked, "The fun never stops."
She heard me and nodded her head,
signaling, "Yes, it does."

Dana once wrote that
her grandma was a songbird.
My mother's voice,
unbroken, sings in me.

Eileen Melia Hession

Me versus Serena

For the last ten years I've been hopin'
To play Serena at the U.S. Open
It's not the trophy and not the cash,
I just want to play at Arthur Ashe.

I've taken the lessons; I've had a coach,
I know how to lob, I know how to poach.
I slice and volley, drop and stroke,
I never fault and rarely choke.

I've played in leagues, I've reached a plateau:
My official rank is a decent three-oh.
Serena's a seven, that's something to fear,
But I still have the feeling I could whoop her rear.

I can see it now; we're on the court,
She hits the net, her serve is short.
Second serve, ace, then more of the same,
Before I know it she's won the first game.

Now I'm up, my serve has spin,
It crosses the net! My ball is in!
I'm thrilled with myself but it doesn't last,
She returns the ball. I blink. It's past.

Sweat pours down my face like rain,
My elbow's sore, my knee's in pain.
Serena's cool, she takes first set,
But I'm confident I can win this yet.

I'm in the zone, focused, tough,
I look at Serena, her arms are so buff!
Her muscles bulge with raging power,
She's hitting ninety miles per hour.

The stands erupt in an awesome cheer
As I feel the ball whiz past my ear,
Geez! Was she trying to hit my head?
I call "FOUL!" (I could be dead!)

The umpire yells back, "Foul denied,"
I guess he's on Serena's side.
We're at match point—almost finished,
We've been playing nearly fourteen minutes.

Now Serena's jumping in the air,
I guess I lost. Quick, where's my chair?
I need a towel, I need a drink,
The crowd is telling me that I stink.

What in the world was I thinking of?
MY scoreboard shouts out love, love, love.
Thank goodness I got to serve the ball
Or I wouldn't have hit the thing at all.

But I'm not discouraged, nor lost my drive
My Grand Slam dreams are still alive.
My tennis days are far from over:
Next year Wimbledon, against Sharapova.

Joan Higuchi

Treasure Hunt

When they climb the rickety stairs
we can no longer manage
to the crawlspace up above
what will they find?

Perhaps some acorns left behind
by an invasive squirrel
we discovered, by the patter of its feet
above our heads

bric-a-brac from various decorating sprees
boxed books we meant to read again
bundled tax receipts, long-past relevance
stacked like scrolls in an ancient cave
a bassinet filled with dusty records
some clothing from our thinner years

and in a far corner, left untouched
the wedding gown I designed myself
stitched by my talented mother
from parachute material
left behind after the war
worn only once
on a fortuitously balmy day
sixty-five years ago this coming summer.

T.K. Hume

Migrations
(for Dad)

Before spring,
we longed for the warmth
of summer but

it was too late this year
to expect a pardon.

Disease had spread
the length of your days.

We agreed on bluebirds
(your form of reincarnation) to
help buffer the loss.

The ducks came back
this spring,
four feathers afloat in the pool
proves their presence

like the nest I found
in the tree
sheltering eggs.

R.J. Huneke

Three To Go

The nest of nerves is disturbed by the saw
A numbing barrage of anxious porcupines
Nearly killed me
Bite after bite, shoot after shoot
Injections raze my mind
Leaves my mouth speechless

The raw stench of heated metal cutting
Driving jackhammering the porcelain bone
My nose cowers
Blood recalls blood, smoke inhale smoke
Cringing the lightning falls
Louder than my screams

My heart clamps still as I pray for a chance
A pause is what I need to cry out speechless
AA AH AH AAH!
Ask me please ask, 'Do you feel that?'
Hot pokers sear my gums
The bastard tooth splits.

Athena Iliou

I Am Autistic

Leave me alone
I am autistic

Tune in to
Multiple
Conversations
Leaves confusing
Hiding in corner, of
My room,
Stories of my brain

Lost footage of words
Rocking for comfort
Can't manage, all import
Emotions of feelings
Storage on files

My autism

can't express my feelings
In my mind...learning to
Manage with balance

Overwhelmed

Words scrambling in waves
Blinded by sight
My body reacts in behaviors
Unacceptable to others

I am autistic,
I lost
Empower of
Expression
In life
Decision

Wisdom
In music,
Therapy

Spoken words

Verbally, or visually
Photos shown or
Object of
Musical instruments

Music teacher
Waits for
College student responds

Teaching choices

Memories,
Feelings,
Singing,
Strumming guitar
Bells,
Drum,
Tambourine or more

Expressions,
Thoughts,
Through
Smiles of
Laughter

Penetrates
Deep to core
Calms soul

Touches heart
Emotionally joy
Shed tears,
Teary eye, of
Progress

Singing in melody
Music time is
Finish

Maria Iliou

Mind Waves

Strolling along the beach
Picking up shells
Sunset scenes
Amazingly powerful
Perfect pictures

Photos shoot
Lens captures
Stories of wisdom

Thoughts are deep,
Far away in your
Own world

Emotions, feelings,
Expressions creeps in
Riding on waves
Overwhelmed

Intensely of impact
Emotional of others
Pain, suffering or
Unspoken words
Visual in

Video format

Time to process

Computer storage
Separates files
In media room, of
My brain

Sharing or hiding
Stories of
Life experiences

Connection, associations
Through conversations arises
Trusting right sources

Traumatically
Memories are buried
Weep, shed tears
Joy of happiness remains

Mind waves
Emerging in beauty

Vicki Iorio

Ode to the Cuttlefish

Splendid Sepiidae
sweeter than Splenda
splendiferous one
cuddle me
coddle me
coo to me

Hold me with your suckers
Don't be tentative with your tentacles
Don't be alarmed by me
there is no need to sepia the waters
I will not outsource your cuttlebone
to parakeets in need of calcium
I like shrimp and mussels,
the same foods you enjoy
I don't mind a little gender bending--
getting flirty in fem colors and polka dots

You are more octopi than fish
I want to swim in your pool,
no pussy of the deep.

Rahul Iyer

Mellifluous strings...

The greatest yet most perfect epitome of pristine humility
Chiseled and coalesced together with the highest virtuosity
Unique while being a true one of a kind artiste most perfectly
An endearing loving Guru sharing everything so generously
By teaching our divine Carnatica Sangeetham kalai patiently
While only meaning well for everyone around genuinely
Top ranking violinist honed by beloved MLV Amma fully
Fantastic violin accompanist to many great stalwarts surely
Living icon and ideal representation of sincere magnanimity
You are my sole beacon and inspiration quite very really
Keep close to my heart our fun time in 2002 at New Jersey
Hope to see you again soon to learn a lot more definitely
Bestowed with numerous awards and titles like Padmashri
Devotee in the revered Lord of the seven hills in Tirupathi
Tears fill my eyes when I hear you play the swarams clearly
Sans any gimmicks replete with spontaneous creativity
Composer and revolutionizer of the highest form of artistry
Gratitude and thanks dear Amma for showing us true bhakthi
As we have all learned so much from your service greatly

Larry Jaffe

I Am Refugee

I am refugee
Nothing is my own

I have no home
No city
No country

I am refugee
I have no food
No clothing
No shelter

I am refugee
I have tears
I have despair
I have misery

I am refugee
My government bombs me
The rebels shoot at me
The United Nations ignores me

I am refugee

Nothing is my own but

I have my honor
I have my morality
I have my love

I am refugee
I am refugee

Jay Jii

Mist Beneath the Tree Line

Mist beneath the tree line
Haze of a summer's night
Clings to grassy fields
Artful kiss of starlight

Haze of a summer's night
Shimmers in the glowing
Artful kiss of starlight
Emerald streams a 'flowing

Shimmers in the glowing
Amidst the crystal pool
Emerald streams a 'flowing
By song of creak and mewl

Amidst the crystal pool
Encircled by the free pine
By song of creak and mewl
Mist beneath the tree line

Ryan Jones

Duality

Two within one
One spread over two
Some know one but not the other
Few know both together as one
Same yet separate
A synthesis

The single two
Presented one way
What is seen conflicts with what is
When the other half emerges
How confused we are
Do we deny

Can we believe
Can we truly know
If one part rules in dominance
Or whether control fluctuates
One rising higher
In circumstance

Evelyn Kandel

Rainy Day Rant

Sometimes reading last week's *Times*
is like eating strained baby food, flat tasting,
had it before and I didn't like it then.
To be honest, having a newspaper delivered
is like being presented with a daily requirement
to be fulfilled, whether I want to or not.
This constant stream of small black letters
begins to feel like water torture, dripping,
dripping words daily and my brain,
poor thing, tired from last night's dreams,
finds the forest of information daunting,
turns instead to something lighter

like the funny papers of my youth, not available
in the newspapers I now read. I should have
gotten married after high school, had five kids,
too busy to read this highfaluting intellectual rag.

Annie Karpenstein

The Beauty of Burl

"Beauty is truth, truth beauty." John Keats from
Ode on a Grecian Urn

Have you ever noticed burl, a bulbous, gnarled
growth covered with bark, protruding from a
tree trunk? Burl even grows underground on roots.
A response to stress. Ugly chronicle of experiences.

Burl, full of contradiction. Rock hard shell. Yet,
extremely fragile. Ready to chip, shatter unpredictably.
Dark, ugly exterior, light and beautiful within.
Sliced razor thin, burl transforms to artistic wood
veneer. Decorative design touch for expensive furniture.

Poachers, looking for quick money, try to surgically
remove burl. Leave tree standing, free of its growth.
It dies without its integral part, domed burden of pain.

Just as my parents' pain, an integral part of them.
Their history, suffering during war, lived on. Ugly
memories stored not only in the mind. Hidden
deep within, at the root of their being, trauma stored
as cellular memory. Encased them in hard shell
of numbness. Froze out their feelings. My feelings too.

94

That trauma passed down to me in DNA. A difficult
legacy I didn't want. Tried to escape its tight cold grip
on the back of my neck. Its icy fingers held me prisoner.

I gathered courage. Confronted burden. Looked deep
within. Tried to understand their life, my life. Struggled to
peel away layer upon layer of pain. Searched for meaning.
Found beauty shining forth.

Nella Khanis

My Camelot

There is no more burning desire
That fueled my Camelot
Losing the last of their fire
Sparks between timbers are caught

Energy – into matter
Falling head first in space
Rearranged atoms better
Fit into my new face

Gathering parts and pieces
Glue me together anew
The old me that nobody misses
The old me that nobody knew

Lois Kipnis

A Kipling Man

He was a

harmonica
violin
playing
played-by-ear
musical
man

snuggling hugging
loved loving
good-natured
gentleman
and gentle
man

joking teasing
twinkle in his eyes
eyes that twitched
if worried
about his family
man

adored, cared for

catered to
Mom's whims
strolled holding her hand
contented
man

chopped/tossed salads
washed dishes
sorted laundry
food shopped
helpful
man

sliced onions on bread
to cure our colds
studied to be
should have been pharmacist
dreams deferred by war
man

did what he could
worked three jobs
cab driver
fruit stand, insurance
door to door sales
man

smoked cigar or pipe
dozed in chair
arms crossed on top of

belly in undershirt
snoring
man

man of his word
man of words
advice from "Gramps"
notes and quotes
from a wise
man

quoted Kipling "If
you can keep your head
when all about you
are losing theirs…
You'll be a Man…"
he was indeed a
man

a Kipling man
walked with rich and poor
met triumph and disaster
held on
picked up the pieces
man

played by the rules
ethical law-abiding
role model, fashion model
dimple on chin

handsome
man

but most of all
a heartfelt man
whose heartbeat
ceased at sixty-six
left us heartbroken
left us
without a violin
harmonica playing
happy birthday phone call
left us too soon
man

Bill Kirsten

J R

They said I need a poem for a contest
I just wrote one last year
or so it seems.
Come on now
I just can't do it.
Oh oh – here she comes J R – that Purple Poet
very much to my dismay
she writes a new poem every day.
She does it, I don't know how
I just know I have to bow
in the presence of the Purple Poet.

Denise Kolanovic

Fluffy King

She has a face like a ferret, with a sneering snout.
Yet, her eyes are mild.
She was a hitter, and proudly displays her garish tattoos
And asymmetrically frosted hair.
Her hoarse voice has an acidic tone
But she could win you with her smile
Or stab you with sardonic innuendos.
She loves to put others on the spot
But will not take criticism well.
She's a hard-boiled child that's been burned.
Now she is trying to make up for lost time.

Varteny Koulian

Captive

You wash over me again ill-timed and unannounced
I lose my footing and you carry me adrift
I wrap my body around your shape to capture all that never was
but you carefully release me then simply slip away.

Mindy Kronenberg

Art & Commerce

She was gnarled and burnished
with the patina of soot and dander,
goat-footed and throned
in the corner of our subway car

A silver pole
her scepter, she raged epithets
at dark suited passengers,
cursed Wall Street

and Trump Tower, her tongue
swollen with venom,
but broke into grateful
and glorious song

when her cup filled
with legal tender

Faith Leiberman

For Those Whom

1.

I know you, knew you
forgotten like holiday bread
consecrated, savored, gone
leaving long shadows of regret.

Did I say forgotten?
There is still some memory of offerings,
small like so many words, longings really
even if abstractly spoken yet meaningful
as air or smoke marked by the presence
of soot, a smudge, a moment's footprint.

2.

Even up north where veracity is authentic,
the season is not white as expected.
Even there, there is reason to answer
predictions with rhetoric and self-doubt.

If only a mind could clear,
with the vigor of a cookie cutter day,
the crying, waiting, wanting

for holidays that hint at self-flagellation;
eager to believe, succumb
to the religion of crying.

3.

I come from the cold with a certain rectitude,
a stumbling, stuttering heart
that learned plagiarism late;
everything sacred, practiced by rote.

Or how holiness and passion repeat like history
and mistakes are easier to forgive than being alone.
After all, everything coming to bloom is still
too close to being cancelled
and come fall, each petalled heart
will not be far enough from crucifixion.

Tonia Leon

Book Mess

That's not a mob in my bedroom
lounging on my desktop, tabletop, laptop
it's an intimate gathering of soul mates and strangers
Pablo Neruda embracing Rainier Rilke
post-modern American poets
siding up to Bill Moyer's *Festival of Life*
wondering whether meaning and nihilism might coexist
Wendell Berry is a sweetheart
he'd get along with anyone
who speaks in a whisper or not at all
and Rabbi Marc Angel
serves up the wisdom of the ages in footnotes to
Saying of the Fathers of which I try to get my nightly fix.
Then there's a pile of poetry books Jose lent me
 – the Swede Sjostrand, the Chilean Zurita,
Yannis Ritsos' *Diaries of Exile*
I'll never catch up
and in the midst of this
library discards I couldn't resist
Durkheim's Socialism
and Rod McKuen's poetry as melodious as his songs
and while the revelry continues
I reluctantly place back on the shelf
poems by my beloved Jose Emilio Pachecho

there are some books which will just have to go
but not *Chaos, the new Science* by James Gleick
it's a book of modern alchemy
where science morphs into poetry

no literary Davos this
but a serendipitous gathering
of writers and their books
for me a heavenly chaos

Paul Lojeski

Fat Darrell Is Dead

i)

He liked doughnuts so much he went to the doughnut
shop every day. He'd rather have been there than on the
beaches up Highway 1, even a nude one full of California
bombshells. Of course, he weighed over 450 pounds then
so, really, going to a nude beach was pretty much out of the
question; besides, at the counter in Jimmy's, he felt right at
home, sliding down a half dozen jellies or chocolate glazed.
His eyes were sad, though, anybody could see that.

He lived in a beat-up house with his angry brother and
mumbling father. None of them cleaned or did dishes so
the place was a fierce mess full of blame and accusations and
longing for the woman just dead and buried. Things weren't
going well, to say the least.

So that sunny day, when the new waitress smiled, he almost
went into cardiac arrest with a mouthful of custard and colorful
sprinkles. His arms flew up and he wobbled on the stool, while
other patrons watched in wonder with doughnut-full mouths
his waging valiant war against gravity's careless certainty.

She called out, "Hang on" and ran around the counter to

throw her slight weight against him, just enough, though,
to steady his quivering bulk. Then she said he was just what
she needed: "A big man to keep the dark away." Naturally,
after wiping the shiny icing off his lips, he offered his service
and a few customers vigorously applauded the sweet scene.

They got an apartment together above his locksmith shop,
above his fuming brother and babbling father who hated
his good fortune. Soon both disappeared in a cloud of hillbilly
rage, accusing him of foregoing family for the favors of a
"snotty whore." He paid no mind, too lost in her slow touch
to care about their jealousy.

However, his mind drifted and business slipped
as he spent days at the doughnut shop, watching her
dance table to table, her singsong "May I help you?"
now the symphony of his life. He ignored the dozens
of doughnuts he ate daily in worship of her, in reverence
rolling over 500 pounds in two months.

But, then, the heroin dude showed up with his money grudge and
waxy eyes blinking forgive-less ultimatums and she packed in a
hurry, leaving him sinking, sailing towards 600 with all hands
on deck. At night, he cursed his flesh burning in this cold place.

ii)

He told me the story the day I sat next to him at Jimmy's
one blue Santa Cruz morning. His eyes were wet and sweat
poured off his mad excess and he said the chest pain banged

like a drum. What could I say? Honestly, I was seriously into
a couple of whole wheat glazed and that hot Costa Rican
coffee and my head hurt from days of decadent dissolution
spurred on by my own lost howling and here I had a stranger
crying his blues on my weak shaking shoulder.

It was too much and a few stools down a white-haired
couple shook their heads slowly in dismay, wishing they
hadn't heard what they'd heard either. But we shared tales
of disappeared women and before long you'd call us friends,
with me cooking the dinner shift at Denny's and him
at the counter every evening, eating his favorite deep fried
chicken and a bucket of fries, shoveling in the grub
with headlights rushing past in the misty California night.

He always followed it with a giant double fudge ice cream
sundae and, more often than not, he'd watch Johnny Carson
in my moldy motel room later, sipping Colt 45.
That's when I noticed he was so big his face had vanished.
.

iii)

All this time later the look backwards becomes, as usual,
a distorted thing: in and out of focus, there but not there,
a questioning of memory's detail, maybe just a concoction
of soft tissue weirdly arranged by high winds at the beginning
of time, who knows, but, whatever, I remember
that fat man in the doughnut shop and I know he died
of a massive heart attack soon after, walking to his
Volkswagen Bug in the parking lot and somewhere

in the molecular buzz of my waking I feel the guilt gnawing
at my guts, guilt for not trying to save him, for not standing up,
for sliding away into years of more disregard. And I think
about all the others I've let down in small and great ways
and I'm left facing the who and what and why of me
stripped of self-deceit and delusion and it's not a pretty
picture. I feel like eating doughnuts, a bunch of doughnuts,
mounds of doughnuts, hell, a goddamn mountain of doughnuts.

Chatham Lovette

(e)xcavate

cripple of your cowardice
i covet you nonetheless
in cavities of archaic text
where you are the most pungent
and

obsolete

stunning trickery of
your innocence
and inexperience
masqued by
the mint articulation
of the only place i know for sure that your hands don't quiver

on paper

i excavate you
over
and
over

trying to discern
who is less despicable

Ed Luhrs

Midnight Station

I watch them move over the marbled ground,
their destinations awaiting completion,
women with bags, men and their suitcases,
inebriates, the dispossessed, star athletes,
foxes with jeweled washboard stomachs,
a dog leading the blind by a leash.
It is almost Sunday in an almost summer station
at the hub of a great city.

I am amused by the man wearing
the super wide brim straw hat.
He is a beekeeper,
and the one standing
by the gate mumbling to himself
looks to me like a bomber.
The bomber and the beekeeper.
I think this is an allegory.
I do not know how to say it all,
but I imagine the forces of good
stored in jars of honey
over which the beekeeper keeps vigil,
but he is nearsighted and cannot rightly fathom
that ominous forces seek to overtake
or destroy the treasure.

The bomber receives voiceless mandates
from an unseen place,
is touched by an insanity
drawing him in smaller and smaller
concentric rings to fix his appetite
on what he most hates.
I am not sure what that exactly is,
but I suspect the storehouses of honey
embody much that he despises.

I wonder who will answer the call
to protect the treasure.
Will it be the crowd of boys
standing across from the ticket booth?
What room is there for diplomacy
or peace negotiation?

A drunken boy exclaims to friends,
"I need to get me a ho!"
It seems there is little hope.
Once the honey is gone,
next will come the pillage
of all that is fertile and green with promise.
All this reality will be the dream of madmen,
I think, but cannot say for certain.

The beekeeper is cleaning his spectacles.
My train departs in fifteen minutes.
I think I will sleep on the train

and dream about the women.

You may think me foolish.

It is true. Never have I worn such a large hat.

Maria Manobianco

Between Silence

outside the rhythm of the beads
there is a silence between prayers
the broken link of anticipation

swallowed breath of awe
sacred moment of blessings
quickened heart of the beloved

between words unspoken
actions not taken
reality and dreams

the fullness of the cup
after the thirst of the run
the silence of rest

there is an empty space
where disappointment burrows
and opportunity slips from reach

there is a light between contemplation
when hope tightens its hold
and life silences no to yes

Joan Marg-Kirsten

That Was Most Wonderful

at a poetry reading
chairs filled the room
a poet read
something he said

my grandfather was there
speaking to me
I am little again
we are at the kitchen table
it's early before others rise
he offers me forbidden treats
black coffee laced with sugar
slabs of Italian bread with butter
he tells me, "go ahead it's okay"
I dunk my bread
some of the butter swirls to the top of the cup
I sip, it's hot sweet delicious
a most wonderful forbidden treat

back home
memories swarming
I think of other times
walks in the park
Grandpa would buy me a Charlotte Russe

small piece of cake nestled in a paper cup
whipped cream on top with a maraschino cherry
not my favorite
but he loved buying them for me
so I never told him

poets read
generously offering parts of themselves
that night that poet never knew what he had given me
it was a road into a time long gone
a slice of my past
a time for me that was most wonderful

Cristina Marie

I am an extra

I am an extra
Unnecessary, but nonetheless here
The one left behind, no one to endear
Just like them but the forgotten one
Left to wander and find her home, trying not to come undone
The one you lied to from the time she was small
Backs turned, vulgar whispers rendered her mind an empty echo hall
Questions avoided, answered tersely, left misguided to misconstrue
Never sharing your other life, the one they all knew
They all knew you lived there too
Except for me, stupid naïve blindly true
I spun and danced, curtsied and pranced
Hoping you'd notice and waiting for my chance
And then you came to us, whistling and smiling
Returning from them happy and beguiling
Short always was your stay
Unfulfilled, my trust again so easily led astray
I stood behind you, looking up to you, pitiful I was, painfully waiting
Wanting you to turn, and believing you would, my need for you to see me never sating
You said to me once you built a beautiful life

But how then could you leave such bright eyes so clouded
with strife
If your love for her was true, steadfast and loyal
I would not have been hidden, my hopeful childish
perceptions spoiled
In the end, standing over you, cold and rigid, you are as you
ever were, gone to me
Anger seeps deeply and fills me, this aching ever failing to leave
Even now that you've left for your last time, buried deep,
you continue to deceive
They all remain unknowingly tied to your misty, foggy truths
But you left not one certainty here to anchor me to you
So here I remain
forever an extra
Unnecessary
but nonetheless here

Michael McCarthy

Kindred Souls

Somehow
from a spark
long ago

a friendship ignites
slowly ripening
by way of good conversation
and those unseen guides

human hands
tender and strong
unfold
entwine
seamless

converted by love
now walking side-by-side
grounded on the spinning earth
ready to explore
endless worlds.

Brendan McEntree

Anodyne

Look at how hard this poem works
to remain innocuous, like Helvetica
signs on hotel pillows,
reading "Soft" and "Firm,"
like the disposable door passkeys
opening to a neutral world of safety,
unthreatening artwork, weighty
commercial furniture and sound-resistant glass,
enveloping you from the threat
of experience of work or leisure,
only the dream-stains of others remaining
on the pillows sometimes haunting your sleep.

This poem doesn't want to preach,
rather, it wants to live like a parkway weed,
born and unhidden, waving at the sun,
ignoring passing cars and insects alike.

Gene McParland

Mark of a Man

What is the mark of a man?
Is it in the power of his arms?
His size?
His dragon rage when angered?
Ferocity in battle?
The amount of money accumulated?
To some it is.

False images really.

The real mark of a man
is in his love;
His gentleness to others,
his beliefs
personal sense of integrity,
honor of self and others,
power of action, not might,
constancy of purpose.

Most of all
it is shown
in how he holds a child.

Florence Mondry

A Moment

If your children complain about the meatloaf,
compare its consistency to grout,
you don't bristle, you laugh with them
despite the hours in the kitchen.
Instead, you make grilled-cheese sandwiches,
forget the stack of compositions to be graded,
vacuuming and dusting already postponed.
You play scrabble on the outworn board,
chuckle at misspelled words and proper nouns,
listen to their favorite cuts from Pink Floyd,
and Black Sabbath on the stereo
as they jockey for attention. You don't yet realize
that this is a moment of grace.

Marsha Nelson

In Clandestine Hours

"Why do you circle the purple loneliness of night and
seldom blush before the sun?"
  ~ Hoxun Huong

The moon creeps up over my sleepy town,
like a barn owl staring into the dark.
Quietness lingers; a thick fog,
that lulls me to sleep,
bone weary and dipped in a coma.
Layers and layers of dreams,
but for some, the night is
a setting for their restlessness.
They haunt bars and strip clubs,
searching for the salve to heal
the mansized hole in their soul.

We were made to create;
to bring forth life.
The mind is a battlefield,
at other times barren;
a frustrated womb;
a walled off city on a hill.
The universe – our incubator,
who will plant the seeds?

Brendan Noble

Story Telling

Hold up, let's take a moment rewind
And take it back to early humans, you will surely find
We've had this primal urge to put our reasons into rhyme
As long as we had someone to listen to us unwind.

A catharsis, a release of emotion
With enough tears to fill up an ocean
And the audience standing there showing their devotion,
That's the ultimate goal of this theatrical notion.

Though things don't always go our way,
Things can go wrong.
Even in the time I'm taking to write out this whole song.
But don't go throwing in that towel or hitting on that gong,
Cause it ain't over till the fat lady sings "ding-dong."

Theatre, just like life, it isn't perfect you see.
It almost never ever happens flawlessly.
And that's perfectly fine cause between you and me,
Would you really want a pre-determined destiny?

The people in your life are characters to engage.
You're your life's director and the world is your stage.
So what if your lines and blocking aren't written on a page?

Spoken word is how we shared things before the modern age.

So stand up, let your voices be heard.
Now that you've got the rundown on the history of spoken word.
It doesn't matter if your story is real or absurd,
It's still the best way to share the lessons you've learned.

Go out into the world and tell everyone your story.
Make it meaningful and rich and full of allegory.
Cause it doesn't matter if your audience size is 1 or under 40
Someone is bound to listen and that's the moral of this story.

George H. Northrup

Lady Sings the Blues

Clarence Halliday, her father,
exits early to pursue a jazz career.
Her mother, Sadie, rides the rails.
At nine years old, their child
stands before a judge
in Juvenile Court, accused of truancy.
Two years later, she is raped
by Wilbur Rich, a neighbor.

At fourteen, prostitution
opens prison doors.
Undaunted when released,
by seventeen she gains
an early glimpse of fame—
what a little moonlight can do.

Hello Count Basie, Artie Shaw.
Even in the satin of success
she must enter hotels
through the kitchen,
use the service elevator.
But at last she pockets
enough money for enough heroin
to stop remembering.

Needles bring her back to prison
twice—
The United States of America
versus Billie Holiday.

Free again,
in one of many idle moments,
Billie pours herself a drink,
ignites another cigarette.

On stage at Carnegie Hall,
she pins trademark gardenias
directly to her scalp.
Bleeding isn't always convenient.

Tammy Nuzzo-Morgan

Daughter, Keep Searching, You Too Will Find Home
for Eliza

I have traveled different countries, all beautiful
and wonderful to visit.
I searched on till I found one I could call home.

I first explored Scotland, with its rich soil. I sadly left
after three years,
carrying an exquisite souvenir in my heavy arms.

Next I traversed Germany, riding a motorcycle in
the open country.
After five years I had my fill of never quite understanding
the language.

Then I roamed for six years in Italy. The mountains and
the lemon trees
were a sight to behold. The sun was what I left with in my
backpack.

Finally, I arrived in England. I knew the language, the streets,
the dawn. This is where I found you, dear one, and for twenty-two
years I have loved living here.

Joan Vullo Obergh

Runaway Ghost Trains

Only when opaque
raven wing blackness
invades dormant senses
realigning time and space,
can you feel the vibrations
of runaway railroad trains,
hear them island hopping
across an unending sleepless night
trespassing like ghosts through walls
bypassing all stations
streaming east to west …
west to east engines
racing too fast to stop
nowhere to escape
no place to hide
as sounds of fantasy flight
liquid as moonlight
spill on touch hungry skin,
while whistle wails in the distance
keen a riff for co-existence
in a dream forsaken universe.
Softly…oh so softly wheels drone
each sound hypnotic, a muffled
far far away clakety clack clakety clack,

mimic and becalm a coward's heartbeat,
as erratic ghost winds
scrape skeletal branches
outside my windows
on a sleep-starved night
when no one else is awake
no one is awake
no one is awake
no one… no one.
Not even God.

Michael O'Keefe

A Litany of Regret

How I got to this place
This point of confounding indifference
I know not
I am left feeling utterly empty
Devoid of purpose
I clutch at strings trying to derive some meaning
It eludes me
I stare blankly at a canvas confused
Perhaps nothing means anything anymore
The act of looking over my shoulder
Has revealed a long stream of wreckage
That I have left in my wake
I have squandered love
I have taken for granted the simple joys
That make a life worth living
I have hurt good people that deserved better
I should not have looked back

Tom Oleszczuk

The Rainbow

I remember it now, a half-century later.
My sister and I were running
along the sidewalk of windowed storefronts,
leading our parents down
the small village's thoroughfare.
Laughing and playing tag,
I suddenly saw bright colors
above a woman's head,
swirling reds and greens to my laughter.
She smiled,
handed me her rainbow!
Mother and Father said,
"No, no, thank you, ma'am"
but she insisted -- it was a joy for her
to give the umbrella to us!

I had it a long time,
until a windy rainstorm
sometime in late elementary school.

Here I am with my own grandkids
running ahead of me in this vacation town,
brightly colored umbrellas on display
to shelter heads with reds, oranges,
yellows, and blues,
just like that stranger long ago.

135

George Pafitis

Growing Up To Be

Up to teen years all adrift
surrounded by disorder, anchored by love,
but all goals foggy, focus splintered.

I kept eye on the ball,
but the ball always rolled out of the picture
distraction set in, drove astray.

Little boy lost, spirited, goals elusive,
not a battle between divinity and devil
more a tale of time age and place.

In maturity time brings and place nurtures,
what is to be, and as I look in a mirror
I see myself looking back.

Despite all the drifting, home is happy,
I am here, the only place to be
since humanness is its own reward.

Bruce Pandolfo

Hemo-glow-bin (Blood Is Electric)

I was young and eccentric.... my blood was electric.
My body surged with the lightning of inspiration.
I'm charged now too, I'll probably burst.
My insatiable ambition grumbles like thunderclouds
pregnant with the heaven's
white-hot, blinding-blue whip cracks.
I bolt forward until I touch-down-to-earth impacts
with hopes to provide quick blasts of illuminating brilliance
to those who glumly grope in the gloom.
YOU are alive. wired. A live wire!
Why are you alive? a light. alight.
Your nervous system is a Tesla coil.
your heart beat is a thunderous roar!
your arteries are power-life-lines!
your blood is electric.
But don't live static!
strike while THAT irony is hot!
fast! flash dramatically,
in jagged staggering declarations,
that cut the sky before your stick your landing.
A crop-circle-tattoo that proved
your brilliant inner burning is meant to make marks too.

Gloria Pappalardo

Life Lesson 101

Let go of yesterday.
It earned a goodbye.
Didn't it stick with you
for 24 hours?

Didn't it tick off 86,400 seconds?
Don't you think
it's tired and deserves
a good rest?

Let go of yesterday.
You hold it too tight
by the hand
when it's ready to
say goodbye.

Maria Pigal

Simple

Every day is the same routine:
You make a joke, I laugh, you smile;
We talk of simple, common things,
The short, sweet time is worthwhile.

And then you're gone—it's time for class:
Where words are many, loud and cold,
Where numbers stack and overwhelm,
Where life is harsh and uncontrolled.

I stumble, fall; fear weighs me down,
No breath, no life; too dark to see.
I scream, I cry; there's nothing left,
I'm drowning in this inky sea.

But then it's silent, darkness gone,
The world has brightened suddenly;
You hold my clammy, shaking hand,
And everything is quiet
Peaceful
Simple as can be.

Susan Pilewski

A Circus Of Subterranean Birds

They are glitter in the dust
the ground swells with their return

cue the clown car, sweep the spotlight
when the circus comes to town

as the Alder's burdens ease
boughs and bark are stripped clean

the air smells of ozone,
the earth plump with buckshot

when the circus comes to town
with its appetite and lies

see the Magpie riding bareback
she has diamonds on her headdress, she is thinking of a lover who
has yet to call her name

a Zebra Finch tames tigers
armed with a corn husk whip and a suet brick

there is no one left to tell him he is in over his head
Sparrows blindly swallow swords, while a Grouse spins plates
of fire

a Downy tern will do a Swan dive
and the soil shall be his bed

cue the clown car, sweep the spotlight
when the circus comes to town.

Davenport Plumber

Clams

The clams are restless tonight.
I feel them stirring under the sand.
It's August and the magnetic moon veils
the tidal river in silver.

The full tide has slowed the flow
over the clam beds.
Could it be the dead calm water
that sets the clams on edge?

Perhaps the gas-flame moon has riled
the stalled, quiet calf-deep water
in ways known only to clams.

Or are my blue-curled toes, squeezing
unwanted sand inside their shells' defenses?
Standing in the moon-pulled tide change,
my soles pulse with the clams' shivering.

Do clams, like bears and wolves, sense
impending earthquakes?
Could it be some vile substance
in the water or a shrill,
sub-threshold, sand disturbing sound?

Or do my feet discern a quiet uncertainty
Lurking beyond our normal senses?

Kelly Powell

Old Caribbean Saying

I.

A woman from Barbados
regally stood outside our office.
She wore clothing of her own

design. Enfolded in the design
of a scarf of rare, raw silk danced
a woman, intentions hidden.

It deepened her color. A sculpted edge
touched her neck, brushed a cheek.
She waited for her husband to arrive.

The lyrical voice of
Aphrodite grown finally wise,
told me an old saying—

               You must not give
   your whole heart to a man, you must
      set a piece apart, keep it
          to yourself, you know.

I.

She, betrothed to a beloved island, beaches
littered with mahogany driftwood; escaped

an arranged marriage. Eloped with a servant,
childhood's pair. Youth ripe, tasted of breadfruit.

Two grains of blue-black sand, clung fast
to a first kiss. Set adrift as Ophelia's seaweed hair.

III.

Into New York's tempest tossed
Like Marie's uncrowned head in a basket.

A naïve love sorely tested,
Differences of birth and art.
Silver and gold remained unblended,
A seductress enters, plays her part.

Steel drums and calypso played,
As old loves were being cast away.

IV.

She wove a tapestry of earth
and blood and sea

Pregnant and alone, from grief

transcended heresies: of America,
Hindu of her faith—

Into the Muslim of a new
husband, found new love.

V.

Island fragrance lingered
in dark hair, looked up
as the husband arrived.

Composed her garment of tears,
entered the car. Bid good-bye.
Set, once again, a piece of her
heart apart. The husband
watched. Clear that he'd seen,
clear he understood.

VI.

*You must not give
your whole heart to a man, you must
set a piece apart, keep it
to yourself, you know.*

As they drove away,
I arranged my simple clothing. Made
my own way toward home.

Pearl Ketover Prilik

I sing the song of my father

I sing the song of my father – every particle of my being
today infused with him as he stands beside me – though
he did vanish one hot August morning – into the sunlight
burning bright on white linen – Though I felt his heart beat
three times under my palm and then stop. – He did not die.

I sing the song of my father – who turned my head to the
first cloud in my first sky – to the wind in the shimmer of
sun-filigreed leaves, to the rippling sea – to the drift of
sand through his fingers as we sit together watching a
tiny fuchsia flag atop his curlicued sand castle tilt, turn
and finally, finally fall, into the inevitable onrushing tide.

I sing – the song of my father who turned my eyes to cobalt
and burnt sienna – educating my sense to the special sting
of turpentine on the clear cold morning air bringing tears to
eyes watching as he stretched and stapled to a wood frame
a pristine canvas holding all possibility.

I sing the song of my father
in the crabs that poked from
the mud on the day on the pier
while he painted and the sun
began to slip below, gilding all
in that silent sacred place to

which he granted me entrance.

I sing the song of my father – to
sun-brown muscle – rippling ribs
to the taste of salt on his flesh
as he carried me close and safe
in herculean arms
far out into
the sea.

I sing the song of my father
to that crinkle-nose-secret-
smile he passed to my mother
as they sang from song-sheets
To his eyes closed in ecstasy as
music shook the walls around us
and I peeked from my own en-
couraged experience to see a tear
trailing his cheek at crescendo

I sing the song of my father as
I feel his hand in mine strong –
ever present – singing in the
shimmer of leaves in a willow
rustling in chestnut blossoms
soaring on the velvet tip of
a blued jay on a clear day
returning caw for call

I sing the song of my father

as he stands watching my ride
on a carousel – light slanting
through high mullioned windows –
calliope playing – platform circling
waiting for me to jump. I jump into
his open waiting arms

I sing – the song of my father
holding my newborn son
in aquamarine waters high
above his head – diamond
droplets falling about them

I sing the song of my father
coffee cups before us filled
again and again – words flying
as red cardinals kindling our
fire of mind and soul

I sing the song of my father
I sing in memory, in reflection
In honor, in dedication and
In love – I feel his presence in
the air that brushes my cheek
yes, in every particle of my being

and though I thought it a wonder
that he left when his hair was
mostly black and his back straight
when he could bend and rise

from the earth of his garden
hands rich with fragrant loam –
though he left still
young enough –

I see him now – hair platinum, the
slightest dignifying slant-stance
shining in the blaze of sun
I see him – I feel him –
for it is from him
in his reverberating voice
that I sing his song
with the life he
lent to me.

Sandra Proto

Cramping My Daughters Style

We arrived at school early enough
So my daughters could play in the yard

I stood a long distance away
With motherly eyes
Watching them race and climb with their friends

The shrill whistle sounded

It was time to line up

My younger daughter walked
Hand-in-hand with her BFF
and gave a look
That stopped me
 From planting a kiss on her forehead

 I blew a kiss

She snatched it from the air
And rubbed it on her cheek
Before settling down with her 1st grade class

I gave an awkward smile
And walked towards my older daughter's line

She was in a circle
With four or five girls in her 2nd grade class

When I approached

They all stopped talking
And glared at me

I circled the outer skirt of their enclave

I blew a kiss

My older daughter quickly caught it
And flicked it behind her ear

I stood looking at my daughters
Disappear into the brick building

And thought

How I was really a mother
Because I had just cramped my daughters style

Orel Protopopescu

Looping Digital Storm
Oliver Laric's "Untitled" Video, New Museum

How fast the baby becomes a fetus
the old man a smiling infant
the talon a hand
the hand a branch
the man a woman
two breasts two gaping maws.

Before we have time
to process anything
in the secret spaces
between our quarks
a fur-clad Eskimo
becomes the hunted bear
Pinocchio a donkey
a child a dog
the dog a god
and joy succumbs
to grief.

Barbara Reiher-Meyers

The Great White One
(Or, the singles scene is like a shark tank)

Oh, Geez! He looks just like
the one that got away!
although he's alive, and sings,
says my poetry is
unaccompanied word,
much more difficult than song.

If this were 20 years ago,
I'd dive into that tank of sharks
to hook this fellow for myself
then try to dull his teeth.

My old wounds have healed,
and, for now, I'll hide inside
my strong shark cage and watch
him circle,
nudge,
and swim away.

Phil Reinstein

Thump Thump Thump

Thump thump thump thump thump
  poll bump   fist pump
crony capitalism catechism on the stump
growing crowds attest their fears so well addressed
he'll wheel and deal make 'em squeal
the Donald at his best

Curb appeal cash unreal fearless never wrong
man of zeal hair so real peerless with his *shlong*
though much to our chagrin
that tan skin and glass chin are so thin
women love him like a pocket full of posies
Megan Kelly Carly Fiorina just ask Rosie

Raise your rump jump for Donald Trump
American will be great again
down in the dumps?   get out and stump for Donald Trump
American will be first rate again
and if you are Mexican or Latin
no California Colorado Arizona Texas or Manhattan

Swimming in the sump with Trump
brimming toxic waste dump Donald Trump
America will be great again
create dominate will be   straight again
America we win

Alphonse Ripandelli

From dreams I awake, again
with familiar feelings of comfort, warmth and calm.
Within me it lingers briefly
a flutter in my depths.
Remnants of tears on my face
betray neither joy nor sorrow
my mind's eye, still blank.
Yet I know it was you
I met in that world between worlds
where truth resides, unbroken and capable
untarnished by the limitations of reality.

Jillian Roath

Do You Remember?

Dedicated to my cousins and the time we spent together

Do you remember our summers?

Do you remember the bumpy road that would lead us to the town of Montauk we loved so well?

Do you remember arriving at Ditch Plains, the very tip of Long Island?

Do you remember the hot sand around our ankles as we reached our determined spot on the beach?

Do you remember the waves and how we jumped into or under every one?

Do you remember the holes we dug and how we made them deep enough to hide in?

Do you remember the wet sand sliding through our fingers and turning into castles by the water's edge?

Do you remember the sun turning the water to gold as we took our last swim of the day?

Do you remember driving home together, still eager for what was to come?

Do you remember the outdoor shower and a brief shampoo and rinse while still in our bathing suits?

Do you remember the hot tub, heavy with foam and soothing to tired muscles?

Do you remember quickly drying and dressing so that the fun could continue?

Do you remember the upstairs playroom and the downstairs room with the bunk beds where we would gather until dinnertime?

Do you remember how, after dinner, there were always enough brownies for everyone?

Do you remember that even though some of us had to sleep on the floor, we always shared the bedroom?

Do you remember falling asleep together, feeling as though nothing could hurt us and the world was perfect?

I remember and I always will.

Rita B. Rose

Swing Set

This is the swing of my childhood
Decaying and shedding its black and blue steel painted skin in
the backyard
Begging to be sat upon once again

At ten I flinched my eyes; swung suspended in air
Kicking high reaching billowy clouds in my dreams
I stretched my legs; the Sugar Maple tickled the tips of my toes
And the warm scent of its sweet sap was delightful to my nose,
I chuckle with joy

Suspended in flight, I moved backward; my heels tapping
Bumblebees feasting pink nectar in the Rose of Sharon
They hum with excitement; social conquerors, keeping up
with my pumping as if it a game
A few bees tag along for the ride, resting on my arm
Soon, they grow bored and with honey baskets almost filled, they
return to the blossoms; their long hairy tongues lapping the
flowery juices

As a teenager, my swing soared even higher in the wind
With eyes shut, I moved to and fro; laughing
The Sugar Maple has gained height and is impossible to reach. I
still manage to enjoy its fragrant bouquet

The Rose of Sharon still faithfully blooms; offering liquid to
its bumble friends

I could feel my legs touching the ground beneath me. I hear the
creak of the swing as it feebly sways
With eyes closed I make a wish to again soar
A subtle breeze moves me; I imagine but never take off
The cool tempered steel is in my hands and I am clutching the
rusted swing chains
Long-standing paint chips are peeling from the moldering frame; a
blue one gently rests on my shoulder; it is how I feel
I want to shut my eyes again; forever, I want to be ten
I want to imagine soaring high with the wind swelling under me
I want to see the Honeybees in flight
I want the Silver Maple tickle my feet
But I am sixty-four and grateful
Grateful, I and my old friend, swing set, can still stand in my
backyard

Marc Rosen

Electrician Wanted

Just woke up, need to bleed the lizard
Legs get the command to MOVE IT!
They do nothing
The alarm goes off, I need to go to work
GET OUT OF BED AND PISS!
The body replies "Nope, fuck you," with no actual words needed

I close my eyes, imagine the room on fire
The heat, the pain, the sheer agony of the flames
I MUST GET UP AND MOVE!
Adrenaline pumping, I THROW myself out of the bed,
Get to my feet, get dressed,
Count out the ten morning pills I need to take
Get in that bathroom, swallow some water
AND FINALLY GET THAT PISS TAKEN CARE OF!

Second alarm goes off.
I have five minutes before I'm late for work.
Fucking brain's on the fritz again.
HONEY! Oh, right, there's nobody else here.
Fucking neurobullshit!
My brain needs an electrician...

Gladys Thompson Roth

No Place for Racists

When the sun came out
the snow made a dazzling backdrop
for birds who came for food and friends:
cocky crimson cardinals, arrogant blue jays
puff grey doves, frisky brown sparrows
resident woodpecker with red cap and striped coat
appeared family in tow.
The changing technicolor scene was riveting.

An abundance of birds at feeders
and on the ground
shared food without a squabble,
proudly wearing their different colors.
Do birds know a secret
that humans have yet to learn?

Miriam Rothermel

The Stillness,
punctuated not by silence
but by a roar,
a din,
a screeching in the distance,
and a yearning–
yearning to see beyond the stillness,
to escape the roar,
to do something–
to just move.
Finally, an exit.

Long Island experience

Narges Rothermel

Harnessed Screams
July-August of 2014

Mourning one sister's death from afar,
other sister on chemo
rough road ahead
Tearless

Children
getting slaughtered here, in Middle East,
in many parts of the world
How can we save our children?

War-monger politicians have no answer
for asked questions,
Why War? Why War?

Newspapers print
part of the naked truth
     I can't process all these

Caught in middle of harsh storms
fog has taken over the mind

Anger has drowned out
every soothing sound

Blurred vision
can't find a helping hand

Harnessed Screams
in need of escape

Solace, such
an empty word!

Ian Rowan

The Thistle

This emblem
From a land of grace
Protector of
The Scottish race

Glorious wondrous flower
Beneath such beauty
Strength and power

By purple heather
Here you stand
Guardian of
This precious land

"O Flower of Scotland"
Where would we be
If not for
The likes of ye

Dorothy Rowlinson

Do You See Me

Chameleon, your eyes conquer me,
and whisper, "Do you see me"?
Sparkling green leaves lie silent.
I ask the wind, and a bird of the night,
        they say "no."

You dance on the emerald leaves
        feasting on insects.
Mother earth seems pleased as
punch watching you eat lunch.

The brown sparrow brings a message
"Chameleons at work, and there is no
        need for pesticides."

Flora, goddess of flowers, bears witness
to the glory of the multi-colored flowers.

Quietly, I search for the camouflaged
        lizard hiding in the garden.

Yes, I see you - the fingerprint of God.

Judith Karish Rycar

The Winter of Our Discontent

As Winter slinks away
its cruel taunts remain
Cruel not because of cold
    there were bone-chilling days
Cruel not because of snow
    great drifts fell to earth
Cruelty born of indecision

Snowfalls melt in spring-like warmth
More cold and snow follow
    again and again
Gaia held captive as
Apollo and Zeus war for control
Until spring finally arrives

Apollo triumphs
warm coats, boots exiled
But Zeus, unconquered, returns
Snow, then warmth, then
bone-chilling rain,
rain and wind savage the Earth

Is this our future?
At the mercy of
the whims and rages
of warring gods

Dana Sausa

Poetry

What it means to me
Being whole mind, body and soul
It' my chi in a nutshell
My energy!
Poetry is what...
What it is?
Is freedom of thought, free to be, no need to erase, no fear on
this page
Private thoughts or personal thoughts but freedom of speech is meant to
be preached
Shared expressed
Respect!
I mean this is my flow it seems
Bold and changed
Bark breaks on a tree and regrows
Well I'm to do the same
Sweat and tears
Bleed into shape
Focused on a mission
Shake this frame
Blood at the roots and at the joists too
Blue in the soul but I'm to be beastmode
Ash to bloom not assuming it's all gloom
Life is funny weird
It's fire and death
While also being water and birth
Poetry is how I deal with life

Robert Savino

Lake Dweller

There's a spot of timeworn sandstone
at the lake where I find sanctuary
sitting amidst sagging branches and sleeping leaves.

Reflections of clouds float slowly
over occasional ripples from soft-blown winds,
in the quiet spill of moonlight.

Shrouds of traveling spirits
change the balance of consciousness.

A single streetlamp flickers and crackles
the fireplace of my imagination.

Home is everywhere and nowhere.
I travel miles to get there.

Andrea Schiralli

That Boy

I look out the window, streaked with rain
Caught in a whirlwind of melancholic pain
Interspersed with traces of bittersweet joy
For in every cloud I find the face of that boy

That boy– the one with the baby-soft hair
That boy– whose embrace makes invisible trumpets blare
That boy– whom I can no longer deny
That boy– without whose love I would die

The days with him were filled with inexplicable bliss
"Gib mir dein Hand" und "Give me a Kiss"
Mornings commencing with White's Lazaretto
Nights rebeginning with soy amaretto

Beach walks and small towns, a week of sheer leisure
To learn how to love you my only endeavor
Garda, Verona, Romeo and Juliet
Thanks for the memories even I can't forget

Speeding down the autoban, what an adrenaline rush
Not caring if life ended beside my Eternal Crush
But we survived – and arrived – at your picturesque home
Where for the first time I lost my impulse to roam

Finally grasped why people do settle down
Being there with my Prince who discarded his crown
Understood why two souls merge into husband and wife
And actually attach to this gift we call "Life"

For never before you have I felt so at ease
Ever-departing like leaves on a breeze
Never letting anyone completely in
But acting on impulse and feminine whim

Once basking in the freedom of my solitude
Now I only find freedom in the loving of you
For when I surrendered, I gave you my all
My reason, my passion, my body, my soul

So here is my Heart– do with it as you wish
Know that each moment without, you are sorely missed
Know you're simply the most beautiful boy that I've ever seen
And with you my realities meld with my dreams

Sophia Schiralli

Emily,
What do you think of, up in your room?
You must have memorized every corner
of the walls
every chip in the wallpaper
or do you pay these worldly things no heed?
do you gaze out the window?
do you wonder how the fresh grass
feels– the morning dew between your
toes– inhale deep the summer soil.
immersed in Mother nature's garden
instead of writing, do you ever long to drop
the pen and live?
do you wonder how a lover's touch
would feel? or is that too much sin?

You know the children love their aunt
like an angel dressed in white
they wish there were more of her
than glimpses from the attic.
you rarely see full sunlight
and rarely feel night's wind
and hail and all the elements,
beating hard upon your skin

you never saw a sunset, sitting without walls
never got caught in a rainstorm
laughing as rain drenched all your clothes
don't you want to feel firsthand
the lightning, thunder, thrills
would you laugh with joy and squeal,
or get scared and praying, kneel?

For although you write poetic
on themes like God, death, love
I promise you the real world
will stimulate your blood
and once your lungs breathe the wet air
and your tongue tastes a blade of grass
you'll glance up at your window
through the other side of glass
and smile to yourself, so glad you took the chance
and though you may not stray too far
you'll always take the long way back

Greg Schroeder

Age

Age, they say, is just a number
Of course, they are all younger
Than I, and much wiser.
They don't feel the creak
Of every joint when I rise
In the morning or lie down
At the end of a long day.
They don't have, yet,
The fading eyesight, dimmed
Hearing, or softened smell.
They also lack the perspective
The additional time has given
To see revolution as evolution,
Movement as fad, and time
As an endless opportunity.

Karen Schulte

Knocked Out

Flashing across my screen a woman
I hardly know, met once, exchanged
pleasantries, some talk about families,
a moment in time now gone except
in a flash her face stares out at me,
a selfie of violence, framed in white gauze,
wrapped and delivered in units of megabytes
to the social network of today's minutiae,
her battered face pictured side by side
with her perfect groomed features,
never knowing what provoked the act—
friend, predator or both in a room of celebration,
subtle layers of rage dissolved in white wine,
innuendoes of whispered rejection,
who knows what else was in the mix—
but there she is in bloodied defiance,
with her image of startling grace.

Ron Scott

The Contestants

They come from all walks of life
Poets submitting their creations
Invitation ... a poetry contest
Five dollars per, twelve for three.

Money not the motivation
First prize translates to a fine dinner (for one)
Participation says *I'm here*
        Recognition.

Judging not an easy task
Reviewing talent greater than mine
My eyes will be joined by others
Willing to agree or disagree.

Rules of judgment on standards:
Meter, metaphor, language,
Rhyme or free verse
Bottom line: prisoners of the subjective.
Pages bleed with emotion
Witness to a sunrise, sunset,
Love, loss, hope and regret
Ingredients of the human condition.

My effort will remain anonymous
I am free to say
Congratulations to the winner,
Hail to the losers!

Nanci Scuri

The Death of the Buddha

And the priests admonished us not to weep as the Blessed One passed on to Nirvana, for how is it possible for any among us not to perish?

So we stood in the dust of the wattle-and-daub town and watched the priests weep as the Blessed One passed on to Nirvana.

And the priests admonished us not to mourn as the Blessed One passed on to Nirvana, for if we exert ourselves, will we not be free from all depravity?

So we stood in the dust of the wattle-and-daub town and watched the priests mourn as the Blessed One passed on to Nirvana.

And the priests admonished us to be still, lest we suffer afterwards and feel remorse, saying "Our teacher was present with us, but we failed to ask him all our questions."

So we stood in the dust of the wattle-and-daub town and watched the priests run hither and yon, scattering birds into the air, as the Blessed One passed on to Nirvana.

And I stood in the middle of the wattle-and-daub town, and the dust gathered at my feet, and the dust pooled at my feet, and I cried as my skin cracked, and my bones split, and my heart broke, and my life's blood poured from me, and out from the hot, dark mud bloomed a single lotus flower.

Cathy Silverstein

Mazie's Burial

Into the ground she goes
curled in her white fur coat
a cat made of stone

Her hideaway is two feet down
I place a round white rock on top
a safeguard from scavengers

Inside the house – a silence
the favored sleeping cushion empty

I keep expecting her to reappear

Keith Simmons

Snoregasm

We've all heard said that sex is fantastic
Even without   the leather   and plastic
If you know how to shimmy and shake it
And remember   not to fake   or forsake it

But soon after,   alas,   he will slumber
But the girls want to double the number
And however hard you try to budge him
You are sure that it won't even nudge him

As he drifts off softly to sleep
you're left there to sit counting sheep
But his snores shake the bed with a roargasm
And you think you'd like one little moregasm

So you slyly wait his next inner rattle
and you slowly climb back in the saddle
Hoping for two   or three... even fourgasm
And succeed with his sneeze and a snoregasm

Harriet Slaughter

Monet's Garden

Where iris bloom
The poppies burst in orange and red
Across from them a bed of tulips
Mingled colors of yellow, blue
With forget-me-nots

Where iris bloom
Wisteria weeps like purple lace
Azaleas show their happy face
And creeping vines intertwine
With forget-me-nots

Where iris bloom
An arching bridge was built
Bamboo stalks stand high as stilts
Lily pads glide among the frogs
With forget-me-nots

Where iris bloom
Monet created beauty there
A riot of color everywhere
A painter's paradise filled
With forget-me-nots

Roger Smith

B Flat & Feel My C Sharp

Strumming hands on her pear shape
sienna stained sucrose,
listening to voice crystallize in my eardrums.
In the most passionate, artistic way,
I clutch her neck
and slide my fingers across the strings that
echo musical moans.
She's fine tuned and stretched out to a sweet capacity
where every noise she utters is worthy of being recorded.
Breathing generates erogenous harmonics.
She is that four letter cryptic emotion,
pounding in chest,
vibrating in my arms
at frequencies that create tension in men's denim.
If only magazines measured beauty by sound.
Sometimes I tap her backside for oomph and dramatic flare.
Affection is a plectrum used to make her hollow body resonate
immaculate acoustics.
Never focused on a number, she sits on the scales of my pulse
whispering the softest tunes,
harmonizing with the music of my soul.

Barbara Southard

Clues and Symbols

Deep under the waters of a Guatemalan lake, ancient
sculptures and five stone docks glimmer among the fish
while satellites from the exosphere expose buried cities,
reminding us what we have now is not forever.

How will we compare the paintings of Lascaux, their
luminous animals rendered on walls by the light of torches
with our own strange markings painted on the concave walls
of train tunnels snaking underground like burrows of rodents?

Who will decode the immensity of zeros and ones?
Or will there be nothing left but fragments of monuments,
strange symbols spray-painted on ruins, mysterious fragments
of earthworks, vague clues to what we held important.

Dd. Spungin

When Lost, Take The Local

Running through my dreams barefoot
Freedom slipping through fingers, ungloved
A local newspaper, my only company
Random thoughts, my salvation

There's a hard edge to the lone life
Cactus-sharp, desert-barren
The lake, bone dry, heaves me onto cracked banks
Ankles bound by broken promises

Sackcloth. You think ashes, but you're wrong
Keeping your secrets in pillows
Scratching initials in the stone of my heart
The depth of despair knocks once

You let opportunity pound, ignored
Breathe, damn it, breathe
No one will discover this place
Steel doors enhance security

Satin stars poke thick holes
The beat softens, patina shines
Listen. It's a strong wind but
No one feels its kiss.

Gregory Vincent St. Thomasino

Conceptus

Small stone cactus
Canker ate its root

Trash it
As the dentist a tooth

The doctor a bosom
Sleep

Arrest this wisdom
Lay chaste its fertile sermon

Hot blood
Scald the bastard notion

Let us hear the damned creeper shriek
Holy Mother of God

Let us crucify this conceptus
Yea Yea cry the masses

And for nails
A list of grievances

Susan Sternberg

Now

It wasn't like this when I was younger.
When I was busy collecting memories
of people and places
dreaming of the next trip or opera or dinner
out and about.
A dandy, a woman of the world.
Running.

These days,
I have given up so much of what identified me,
what I identified with
my rituals even.
It's not that I've tried to do this.
It's been happening on its own
like a change of season
like dead leaves being pruned from a tree in a breeze
gently falling off.
My pulse has slowed.
I feel the silence.
I'm vibrating in harmony with the earth
now, and at peace.

I wonder about the earlier me –
the one that was so driven to experience and excel.

What a burden the try was,
what an obstacle to discovery that path.

I think of Mr. Prufrock,
a man I first met in Sweden
when I was as far away as I could imagine at the time.
I know that my pants are no longer a fashion statement
but rolled
draped loosely over my body.

But my mind.
My mind is finally alive, fecund,
expanding exponentially into space.

Ed Stever

Confined

I'm living in the slum
of my mind, broken bottles,
rusted cans, fish skeletons,
pustulating rats, cockroaches,
maggots, lusting lice,
as a man in a filthy overcoat
and piss-stained pants
sits, leans against
a back alley wall.
He wants out,
out of these confines,
this lurid hell, with all
its demons and spent sperm.
He begs my pardon, begs to go,
and I, of the crooked-tooth smile,
simply croak, "No."

Kate Dellis Stover

Another Life

She walked the streets of the neighborhood
That had been her home since she was a child.
It was dusk.
She made her way down the sidewalks, alone.
She could see into the brightly lit kitchens
Where mothers cooked dinner.
They placed their babies in highchairs,
Set the table
and watched for their husbands to pull up in the driveway.
In no time, the whole family was in the kitchen.
They had taken their places at the table and began their evening
meal.

She passed house after house,
The lights up high, everyone talking and eating.
She could only imagine what they were saying,
But she felt the warmth of their togetherness.
She was a stranger to all of them.
She lived in exile just down the street.
Always, as she turned the corner toward her home,
She whispered out loud the same question:

2

"Will I ever have one of those?"

A life.
That was her whispered secret.
That close-knit group around the kitchen table,
Born of the same blood,
Bound together by a love, honest and whole.
They didn't know what they had.
It was so natural, so pure, that it defied definition.
Their happiness was not full of excitement.
It did not beg for attention.
It was simply present as long as all of them were there.

She was a voyeur.
Nothing more, nothing less.
She had a voyeur's imagination.
In her mind's eye, she lifted the babies up to seat them in
their chairs.
Chubby and white, they smelled of freshly picked apples.
Too soon, she had to let go of them.
She would have sung to them.

3

She would have held them for hours.
The real mothers so busy with their tasks
Had no idea that a short distance from their kitchen window
Was a young woman who would have given anything,
Everything to be on the other side of the glass.

Jose Talavera

Being in this room always brightens the day
Always with a smile we welcome everyone
Reading our poems so that all of us can hear
Dwelling into the stories of the past year
Sharing the memories and creating more

During these times we rejoice in our craft
After it's done we gather and say
Year after year, happy bards day

Gayl Teller

Worn-Out Walking Shoes

Who would have thought when I saved them
with an unwitting toss to this garage corner,
I would come to savor them later,
with their stained tongues loosened

over maws opened wide by many ingested miles
I walked, some alone in abounding sun seeking vision,
sometimes the inventor of my own cold, curable night,
or even on the underside of joy's hush, the great rush,

or felt their scraping down sudden drops
I never saw coming. What sloughed-off skin—
dried sweat-tears salt lick—defiant hues,
what dirty-sweet crumbs-grit—fur-blossom-bug bits—shit

got ground into the honeycomb fibers, the sole-treads,
what untraceable flecks make such a rich journey mulch?
Ground in, our grandkids' sweet ice-cream drippings
mixed with the rising beach sand, while we rolled

our bocci balls and roared with the untamed wind,
with feather barbs from the Flamingo Gardens Rescue Center,
where Mike and I hand-fed ibis and spoonbills
in the haven for the broken-beaked, the broken-winged,

and I walked among them, picking up the feel of their beings,
and from the company of each friendship, a little ship
moving me deeper into the currents of humanity,
as I tapped my feet and shook to the peppery beat

of the Dutch folksinger in the outdoor concert
at Grand Place, on our vacation in Brussels, last summer,
and exchanged addresses with the jovial woman akin to me,
photographed her baby with the dark eyes like ripe cherries,

ground in, the harbored tears of the lost Korean woman
we walked with for miles, till we found her hostel,
talking all that warm dark while without the same language,
with tears soaked up from strangers weeping together,

strangers from all around the world, stunned and aching
over naked human cruelty, depicted at the Anne Frank House,
so many tears, such living testament to human compassion.
Who would have thought how everyone who's ever moved me,

from everywhere I've ever been, in these worn-out walking shoes,
would come home with me, rubbing through the skin of my life.
Who would have thought they would become like a child,
moving around inside me, keeping me awake at night.

Hope Terris

13th November

Lying in the blood of another
I breathed in the acrid smell of
Fear and gun power

I was an animal only
Relying on instinct and
My cowering heart

I hid under a stranger's
Bleeding body feeling
The moment when his soul rose

And there near the ceiling
Amongst our killers
Was a reluctant dance of souls
Turning back for one
Last look

They saw me hidden and afraid
And whispered
"It's okay."

Maria Torres

Conscious Sedation

I just want a happy home
So my soul won't have to roam
In and out of this conscious sedation
Monotonous day to day shit
Wake up and relive the pretty little lies
That please the eyes
But break my spirit a little bit more each day
Knowing where I want to be
Longing to be free
Stuck in this purgatory suburban dream
Nightmare to my joy
Insanity is this routine
Conscious sedation now my only release
Shiny floors and sparkling glasses
Filled with bitter sweet liquor and empty promises
The sound of the silverware against the fine china
Shattering my insides
Cutting through my nostalgia
Leaving my soul agape
This emptiness so full
A cold draft slipping in from under the door
Right through me
Numbing all that's left
Sleepy hollow now an avenue inside my heart

Can't seem to shake this feeling that sets in after dark
I want to run away somewhere very far
Disappear into the night's sky and lay beside the stars
Let the Moon guide my way
Let the Sun open my eyes
Let the Earth pull me closer
Let the Sea wash away the old
Everything anew
A promise I made unto you
It will come true
I just want a happy home
A place to call my own
Free of this conscious sedation

J R Turek

Tools to Use to Crush a Walnut

You could try a hammer
especially after you dump the junk drawer
on the floor and can't find the blasted nutcracker
or try a pair of pliers if the jaw will open wide
enough for the nut head to fit in, then slam
the handles together.

You could try to pry it open with force, jam
a flathead screwdriver into the seam and twist
it like a knife in the throat of your enemy.
If that fails, place the nut in a vice, crank it
until it cries, but wait – you'll have shells
imbedded in the heart and you could be
accused of murder.

Set up a video camera and watch that squirrel
that hops along the fence pole annoying the crap
out of your dog, take notes on how he does it.
Of course, you could use a DeWalt 20 amp
reciprocating saw with a diamond-point blade
but even that won't satisfy your craving for power.

In the end, get a friend to hold the walnut
while you jab it with a sharp chisel. Steady

your hand best you can but if you can't trust
your best friend not to flinch on you,
what good is she.

When you give up hope of getting to the heart
of the problem, consider tools to use to crush
a spirit. A single evil act will do.

Don Uhrie

Traffic

There is no end, I
Feel like I'm stuck in
A huge parking lot with
No way out but up.
Since I don't see any helicopters flying
Overhead with a rope ladder, I'm
Destined to sit this out, my
Thoughts drift like waves from
One thought to another.

My father, long deceased, so
Many years have passed. I wonder how life
Would be different had
He survived his self-destructive ways. What would
It have been like to have his guidance
When I am walking in the dark. Maybe
Life would have been worse for us both, especially
If he had kept drinking, coming home inebriated, spewing
Incoherent phrases and obscenities.

The traffic begins to move and jolts me
Back into the present, the reality of now, stuck
In traffic...fatherless for thirty-four years. I feel
An emptiness that expands inside me like a balloon
Being inflated. Again I go numb and simply
Wish my life had been different.

Pramila Venkateswaran

Next Year in Jerusalem

1

We're back among our people,
Our feet at last planted in ancient soil, now bloodied.

We've answered the call of Zion
Among anthems of bullets.

We hear them through the muezzin's call
And from shabaath to shabaath.

We strain to hear the sacred words
Spoken before our lifetime, words
Lost often in air ripped by blasts.

2

We're back to a brown land;
With headphones on,
Listening to Bollywood songs,

We grow gladioli and roses
Of Malabar, sing Malayalam songs
Mixed with Hebrew to our children,

Keep our ears trained to a peace
We once knew, become jasmine
In the Negev.

Jennifer Marie Vento-West

Love Reflects Lust

Lust
needs sex,
always thirsting, wanting endlessly.
Throbbing sensations flow righteous.
Sweat heated the lying souls.
Impurity gathered.
Dreams ripen into pieces, tearing dreadfully
circling.
Lust wants
Love
wants lust.
Circling dreadfully
tearing pieces to ripen dreams.
Gathered impurity.
Souls lying the heated sweat.
Righteous flow sensations, throbbing
Endlessly wanting, thirsting always.
Sex needs
Lust.

James P. Wagner (Ishwa)

Goodbye, My Hogwarts

In a post-Harry Potter world
All kids dream of getting a letter
That promises to whisk them away
To a school of wonder and magic.

By the time I first saw you,
I had long been beyond
The hopes of such a letter
A sarcastic angsty teenager
Newly graduated from high school
Fed up with the idea of more school
Wanting instead to focus on my
Dreams of becoming a best-selling writer
No more time or patience for sitting in a classroom
Only going to classes to give myself more time
To nail that one best-selling novel that would make sure
I never had to worry about money again.
(oh youth.)

Sure, the campus was beautiful, by the river
Great view
Historical mansion
So spending time here wouldn't be so bad
Not so bad…

Like Hogwarts, you were beautiful
Like Hogwarts, you taught me magic
The professors, the clubs
The fellow students, showing me
My potential
My ability to do things
I never imagined I could
Like a clueless Harry Potter
I walked through those doors on my first day
Not knowing what to expect.

And now, more than 12 years later
Look back at the degrees there
And realize that these were not the valuable things
It was the experiences I had
Through the various clubs and organizations
The things I learned in the classrooms
With some of the finest professors out there
The people I met, the friendships I made
The love of my life
My future bride
All of these things, irreplaceable.

And although it's been years since I graduated
And although your doors may be closing forever
I will never forget the magic I learned
In my time there
Studying with the other witches and wizards
Of my generation
Who now go forth to cast spells

On this world.
Goodbye, my Hogwarts
Mischief managed.

Margarette Wahl

Scent of Memory

For Michael Nappo & family

"Paint tomorrow with today's brushes" Valerie Griggs

My first crush in high school
now in his 40s lives on,
holding onto life's changes.
He carries its burdens and losses.
I carry some too.
He paints walls and ceilings
with his late dad's brushes.
Opening cans of paint
he holds his father's spirit,
smells it in memories.
It carries him through tomorrow.
For me, paint will never be
the same again.

Herb Wahlsteen

Beauty of a Cloud

A gilded cloud,
I fill the sky
with beauty – proud
I change, don't die.

I'm quite carefree
while floating round.
Who bothers me?
I can't be bound.

No fears at all,
no one will care
if I'm short, tall,
or how I fare.

Blown by a breeze,
now here, now there,
above the trees,
not hurting anyone, anywhere.

Virginia Walker

English Teachers Invade Vegas

Not a good match. I keep thinking of Gwendolen Harleth
as I pass the crowded tables on my way to my room.
In myth I know Yudhishthira of the *Mahabharata.*
Perhaps the sleepless souls before the spindly bandits
with garish signs have never read the great books.
My room is at the end of a narrow hall with a mirror
but my reflection never appears ghostly before me.
Then as I see the long number, my wavy form pops.
My room is a Japanese Porn of mirrors and steel.
Lifting curtain and blind I find a jutting temple
obscuring all but reflective lights. I need to eat before I die.
The walk back ends in a pricey burger overlooking bandits.

A.M. I grab an ersatz bagel and lox while walls of screens
blink races worldwide and immobile shapes sit in rows.
Marble slipperiness pursues my feet all the way to a lecture.
Between the lecture hall and hotel are pools magnificent
yet uninviting in the chill daubed on a November desert.
In a break I confer with like kind. She speaks my words,
my ventriloquist's dummy dressed for English Lit.
Why would you come here if you are not interested
in naked women (where are they?) or expensive shows
(that figure scratching at her pelvic bone on screens
above the check in), or to lose in those cramped tables

(yes, where was the space in Bond films?), or to **die?**

I have to agree with my alter ego, but she is much neater,
her hair bunless and sleek, her manicure perfect pink.
Another lecture, another hall run and lunch -- famous gumbo.
No one really sits, only perches, ready to run at chance.
For some the die is cast. They bring their own snacks
and keep genuflecting while the tumblers run awry.
Others that I meet on the bridge over the avenue,
playing at poverty, even the stink of it, get some coins
until the police sweep them away. High rollers must be
way on top where the roller coaster screams between
fake skyscrapers. At least the Thornton Wilder talk
brings me back to ground in this town of forged lore.

George Wallace

A Radio Believes It is Singing This Song

a river looks up at
the sun -- I am fire,
says the river, I am
the mountain in my
belly, rumbling stone
by miraculous stone
to the sea.

Mira! says the river --
Mother, look at me!

But the rain has no eyes

Jeffrey Watkins

Marie

For Marie Klayman

if I were given the power to create a new world,
as sure as you rise each morning and your golden locks unfurled
I would start with my sun being your radiant smile
its rays would be the hue of your hair's golden strands
its warmth the very touch of your soft and delicate hands
at night your eyes would be its moons and all the heavenly pearls
yes, your eyes would be the nocturnal lights beaming in my world
your perfect body would give my world its various shapes
and forms
your laughter its winter winds and welcomed summer storms
in my world your beauty would blanket its every mile...
yet to begin my beginning my world would begin with just
your smile

Charles Peter Watson

Classic Devalue

O long road ahead
your miles counted
traveled
by a mortal tread
of radials preyed upon
by debris of both worlds,
gradual odometric changes
each block gone around,
in, through, gripped
by elements of wear,
tearing a byproduct in one's integrity.
Annual ring or wrinkle earned
each of every thousand miles, a loss
in value if not vintage, lament for unpopularity.
Before long, more digits on the clock than the price tag.

Marq Wells

Metaphoria

It was several hours
after we had returned home
from a grand day at The Circus
that I observed an evil-lipped clown-thing
with eight legs crawl out from beneath
our blanket and start to consume my wife.

Strangely enough,
there was no blood,
only a moist smacking sound
and the clown-thing's glowing red eyes
that kept me pinned to the bed
helpless, mesmerized.

This was no nightmare.
The spider-clown-thing was very much alive
and guess who was next on its menu?
So what to do?

Once I realized that the clown-thing
was actually a metaphoric extension
of my latent anxieties,
it simply vanished into thin air
leaving no trace.

214

I breathed a sigh of relief
as I watched my wife sleeping fitfully beside me
although as she rolled over onto her other side,
I noticed that her left arm
had been torn from her shoulder.

It was then I began to scream.

Maxwell Corydon Wheat Jr.

Orb Weaver

Araneus emerges under August stars.
Her thread, a silken lariat in the breeze,
catches on the lawn chair,
a bridge she battens down.
She spins gossamer spokes,
orbits support lines around the inner regions
and around the outer, viscid trap lines.
She waits in the center of her universe.

Jack Zaffos

I Ride On This Train

I ride on this train.
I get off again at the
same time,
same place,
and I see you once again
and I wave and you wave
and you're happy to see me,
it goes on and on
as a dream vision
on a spring day.

Then I enter the train again,
again I ride alone
until the train pulls into the station
and again the smiling,
and again the waving.

A smile sincere
and a wave so well-meaning
that may someday
release the gate of separation.

And the ride continues
up and down the line

217

until it reaches the station,
and the train stops,
the doors open,
the mouth smiles,
the hand waves
again one more time.

How long for the walls of division,
how long for the screen of illusion,
how long for this endless streams of assumptions.

The barriers that keep us apart,
they can fall away,
stepping lightly we can walk
down the platform stairs
joining, walking in a meadow.

Or perhaps they will not,
what happens then.
The trains will run again,
but the hand suddenly will stop waving,
and the mouth will suddenly stop smiling.

Lewis Zimmerman

Secrets

What we have, none could know
like Miss Annabelle and Poe

Bliss unbound, mine and hers,
In my slumber re-occurs

Pleasures greater and grand
than what days afford on land

This for us nightly waits
just across the twilight's gates

To the shore and she's there,
shells and seaweed in her hair

Brightest smile ever seen,
tail of iridescent green

So we glide through the brine
sharing love and joy divine

Bubbles rise, currents drift
bringing every lovely gift

When our time nears an end
toward a quiet cove we trend

Sweet repose there we take
and alone at morn I wake

So the question would seem:
Is that world or this the dream?

About the Authors

Lloyd Abrams a retired high school teacher and administrator, and an avid recumbent bicycle rider and walker, has been writing short stories for close to thirty years. Lloyd's poems and stories have been published in a number of anthologies and publications.

Esther Alian is a Long Island-based poet and writer. She has lived on 4 continents and her writing reflects the centrality of human experience transcending religion, culture, and walk of life.

Donald E. Allen is an author of both fiction and poetry. Don joined the Bards Initiative in 2013. He is also a member of the Performance Poets Association, the Nassau County Poet Laureate Society, and the Academy of American Poets. Don is the author of a poetry collection, *April 1861*, and a novella, *When the Ripper Calls*.

Sharon Anderson has been published in many international and local anthologies and received a 2014 Pushcart nomination. She is the author of *Sonnets Songs and Serenades*, and *Puff Flummery; Chutes and Ladders* is forthcoming this fall. She is an advisory board member for NCPLS and a PPA co-host at Oceanside Library.

Peter Arebalo Mc2 is a poet and spoken word artist hailing out of Long Island. He is the host of the Muse Exchange and a regular on the New York open mic scene. His work offers a journey through intense vulnerability, presence and self-discovery.

Works by **Frances Avnet** been published in *The Arts Scene, The Narrateur, Creations*, the *Bards Annual 2013, 2014, 2015* and *Rescued Kitties Two*. Currently she blogs on East Meadow Patch about being an historic re-enactor.

Bob Baker is a former retail store manager, insurance support manager, and early on worked a stint on Wall Street. In all of those jobs, he felt like a square peg trying to fit into a round hole. When it comes to writing, he doesn't write for a living, but rather he writes to live, to exist, like most people live to breath.

Julie Baldock is originally from LI, now resides in a tiny town at the base of Mount Rainier in Washington. When not writing poems about feminism and body image, she teaches high school English and works at a non-profit that specializes in on-time graduation for foster youth in the community. julieisthebeesknees.wordpress.com.

Sybil Bank, a member of the Port Washington Poets Circle, award-winning prose and poetry writer whose publications include *Long Island Sounds, Oberon, PPA, Paumanok Interwoven, Whispers and Shouts, Toward Forgiveness*. Her first book *River Over Stones* was published in 2014. She is one of the Three Poets.

Patricia Z Beach is pursuing her passion for writing after an established career in transportation capital program management. Patricia holds a BA in English from St. John's University and an MS degree in Construction Management from NYU/Polytechnic. She resides on Long Island with her husband and daughter.

Antonio Bellia (Madly Loved) is a renaissance man who has traveled many paths, a man of deep sentiment drawn to performing arts, who has acted and danced throughout his lifetime, and always compelled to express his emotions and experiences in the form of poetry. He is translating his poems from Italian into English.

Don Billings is a retired special education teacher. He enjoys gardening, folk music, opera and Broadway, and occasionally writes a poem. He is the author of *From Within*.

Maggie Bloomfield, a psychotherapist/writer/performer and Emmy-winning lyricist for Sesame Street. Publications include *The Southampton Review (TSR)*, *PoetryMagazine.com*, *Grabbing the Apple*, *Psychoanalytical Perspectives*, *The Montauk Anthology*, and *Suffolk County Poetry Review*. She is one of the "Poets of Well-Being."

NYC Native **Peter Bové** currently resides in Texas making his documentary *The Peyote Road* about the Peyote Ceremony of the Native American Church. His recent Solo Exhibit of Fine Art at the Alliance Francaise received rave reviews. A collection of 57 poems titled *Souls Weep* in the Ekphrasis style is forthcoming.

Richard Bronson is on the faculty of the Center for Medical Humanities, Compassionate Care & Bioethics at the Stony Brook University Medical Center. He is on the Board of the Walt Whitman Birthplace and Long Island Poetry Collective, facilitating its weekly workshop.

Alice Byrne is a psychotherapist in Huntington. She holds a BA in English and MSW from Adelphi University where she also studied dance. She is a mother and grandmother and has written poetry since childhood. She is a frequent presenter and workshop leader for therapists.

Paula Camacho moderates the Farmingdale Poetry Group. She is President of the NCPLS www.nassaucountypoetlaureatesociety.com. She has published three books, *Hidden Between Branches, Choice, More Than Clouds* and three chapbooks, *The Short Lives of Giants, November's Diary,* and *In Short.*

Anne Coen is a special education teacher who has been writing poetry since the 1970s. Her work often contains wry observations on conundrums of everyday life. Publications include *Bards Annual 2014* and *2015, PPA Literary Review #18* and *#19,* and *Thirteen Days of Halloween 2014* and *2015.*

Joe Coen is the other half of a poetic duo with his wife Anne. He is the father of a free spirit and physics major. He has been published in *Bards Annual 2015* and *PPA Literary Review #19.*

Arleen Ruth Cohen is an artist and a poet. Publications include *Creations Magazine, Whispers and Shouts,* and her first poetry book, *Over Pebbles Into Pools,* which is forthcoming this summer.

Latisha Coleman also known as Mz. Conception is a poet, author, host and actress from Queens, NY. She is 23 years old and has won multiple awards and recognition for her poetry. She published her first book, *Poetic Destiny,* in March 2015. She hosts her own open mic in Queens.

Christopher Collins is a 24-year old poet who explores all types of poetry genres and who strives to write about any subject that can affect the inner most human emotions. He is honored to be a part of *Bards Annual 2016*.

Lorraine Conlin is the Nassau County Poet Laureate (2015-2017). She is involved with many LI poetry groups and workshops and published in many anthologies. Her first poetry collection, *Collage* (Local Gems Press) will be out soon. She is a US Customs Broker, a breast cancer survivor and a "student of life."

Jane Connelly is an artist, writer, graduate nurse and former legal assistant who lived in Guam before moving to LI. She placed 1st Runner Up in the *2016 LI Light Poetry Competition;* 2nd at the *2015 LI Fair Poetry Contest, Old Bethpage Village.* Recent publications include *The Avocet* and *Nassau County Poet Laureate Society Review.*

Lisa B. Corfman is a mixed media artist centering on origami. Lisa has two origami books in the works, and hopes to write *The History of Origami.* She holds a BFA in from Endicott College and an Advanced Certificate in Marketing from Dowling College. www.RockyArtsUnfolded.com.

Alexandra Curatolo is 10 years old; she is a 4th grader at Norwood Avenue Elementary in Northport, NY. Alexandra enjoys dancing, baking, horseback riding, and writing. She also loves all things Harry Potter.

Jeanne D'Brant is a holistic physician and professor of Biology and Anatomy. Her works have appeared in numerous scientific and alt med journals, as well as yoga and Feng Shui publications. She is a world traveler with visits to 66 countries on 5 continents; her poetry focuses on imagery of distant lands.

Caterina de Chirico is a French and Spanish teacher, yoga therapist, artist and children's book editor. She makes her home in the beautiful seaside town of Northport.

Douglas Dennison has been a son, student, Marine, husband, father and salesman. He has occasionally found love and as often lost it. All have informed his poetry.

Linda Trott Dickman is a life-long learner, a seeker of rhythm from trains on tracks, to cicada serenades, to the deep thrum of a Harley convoy. She is a school librarian. She and the love of her life make their home on LI where they both grew up on opposite sides of the tracks.

Sharon Dockweiler is a poet and writer living in Bethpage, NY. She has a degree in English Literature and a background in Marketing. She is a spokesperson for people with eating disorders and mental illness, as she suffers from and triumphs over both each day.

Peter V. Dugan is one of the illegitimate feral offspring of the Beat Generation. He lost his mind in Coney Island, and Far Rockaway broke his heart when they tore down Playland and stole the memories of his youth. He hosts Celebrate Poetry, a reading series at the Oceanside Library on LI.

Vivian Eyre is a poet, a painter, and poetry advocate on the North Fork of Long Island, NY.

Elizabeth Fonseca is an avid traveler who has lived in such countries as Italy, Turkey and the United Arab Emirates. Her poetry and prose have been published in the anthology *A Taste of Poetry* and the *Travelers' Tales* anthology series, among others. She teaches at Nassau Community College on LI, NY.

Kate Fox is a mother, a breast cancer survivor, and author of *My Pink Ribbons* and *Hope*. She has been a contributor to *Great South Bay Magazine* since 2004. Her work has been published in several anthologies. She received the 2014 Bards Humanitarian Award for her work for Breast Cancer Awareness and the American Cancer Society.

Shilpi Goenka is a graduate student of Biomedical engineering at SUNY LI. Apart from being a researcher; she is an avid artist, poet, writer and spiritualist. Publications include *Bards Annual 2014* and *2015* and *Suffolk County Poetry Review 2015.* *silentsculptor.blogspot.com*

Jessica Goody's work has appeared in numerous publications, including *Reader's Digest*, *The Seventh Wave*, *Event Horizon*, *Chicken Soup for the Soul*, and *The Maine Review*. Her poem "Stockings" was awarded 2nd place in Reader's Digest 2015 Poetry Competition.

Aaron Griffin, also known as "Super Train Station H," graduated with a degree in Creative Writing in 2015 and likes trains more than most people.

Maureen Hadzick-Spisak is a retired Reading and English Teacher. Her poems have appeared in many anthologies including *Whispers and Shouts; Paws, Claws, Wings and Things;* and *Sounds of Solace.* She is a nature photographer, but poetry is her first love. She is a member of the Farmingdale Poetry and Creative Writing groups.

Sylvia Harnick is a member of the National League of American Pen Women admitted as poet and mixed media artist. Publications include *PPA Literary Review, Whispers and Shouts, Toward Forgiveness,* and *NCPLS Review.* Her creative process in poetry and painting is similar, using imagery, metaphor, and enigma.

Nick Hale is a literal and metaphorical hat collector. He is the vice president and a co-founder of the Bards Initiative. Originally a native of Huntington, Nick currently lives in Northern Virginia where he leads a poetry workshop group. Nick is a manager, publisher, and editor at Local Gems Press. Nick's first collection of poetry, *Broken Reflections,* is available from Local Gems Press. He is currently working on two upcoming collections of poetry: *30 Pieces of Silver* and *Public Education.* Nick's enjoys reading his poetry live. He doesn't get to as often as he would like, but can usually be seen wearing his trademark bowler hat while doing so.

Robert Michael Hayes has been writing for a little over three years. His works have appeared in publications such as *Avocet, Odyssey,* and *Long Island Quarterly.* He is a proud member of the PPA, LIWG, and the Farmingdale Creative Writing Group.

An eight-time Pushcart Prize nominee, **George Held** publishes regularly both online and in print. His recent books include Neighbors 3: The Water Critters, animal poems for children, illustrated by Joung Un Kim, and Culling: New & Selected Nature Poems.

Gladys Henderson's poems are widely published and have been featured on PBS Channel 21 in their production, *Shoreline Sonata*. She was the 2010 Walt Whitman Birthplace Poet of the Year. Finishing Line Press published her chapbook, *Eclipse of Heaven.*

Judith Lee Herbert returned to poetry after a successful career. A graduate Cum Laude in English Literature from Columbia University, she has been published by *Long Island Quarterly* and *motheringinthemiddle.com*. Judith has strong roots in LI and currently lives in NYC with her family.

Eileen Melia Hession likes to write and she usually does it in rhyme. She thinks there's a need for more humor in this world and her writing reflects this. She is a lover of tennis and running and Jujyfruits. Her work has appeared in many (but not enough) publications.

Joan Higuchi, winner of consecutive first place awards in the PPA haiku contests, has recently been published in *Avocet, The Long Islander, The Long Island Quarterly Centennial Issue, The Lyric,* and *Odyssey and Prey Tell* (an anthology developed for the support of the Owl Moon Raptor Center).

T.K. Hume is a caregiver and has been writing since she was 18. She is currently working on her own book and is pursuing a career in the medical field. Her poems embrace heritage, love and love lost.

At age nineteen, **R.J. Huneke** traveled across the country from New York to California in a dilapidated van with no brakes or heat . . . in winter. It was there that he began to write his first novel. His debut for a major publisher, the sci-fi thriller *Cyberwar,* came out in 2015 and is in bookstores.

Rahul Iyer is an active avid animal activist, animal lover, composer, critic, foodie, poet, singer, and writer residing on LI for 30 years. He has over 10 years of professional musical experience. As a writer, his craft was honed under guidance from The Wheatley School's best English teachers, School Within a School (SWS) program.

Athena Iliou is the daughter of Maria Iliou. Greek autistic abstract artist and actress, Maria's paintings and Athena Maria drawings are displayed in *Joyful Expressions: A Vision of Autism* art exhibit featuring the work of children and adults with autism.

Maria Iliou is an autistic artist, poet, actress, director, producer, advocate, and host. Maria's been published in *Perspectives, Bards Annual 2011* and 2013*, and *Rhyme and PUNishment.* Maria is host for Athena Autistic Artist, which airs on public access tv and hosts the radio show, *Mind Stream The Movement of Poetry and Music.*

Vicki Iorio is the author of *Poems from the Dirty Couch*, Local Gems Press, and the chapbook, *Send Me a Letter*, dancinggirlpress.

Larry Jaffe was the poet-in-residence at the Autry Museum of Western Heritage, a featured poet in Chrysler's Spirit in the Words poetry program, co-founder of Poets for Peace (now Poets without Borders) He was awarded the Saint Hill Art Festival's Lifetime of Creativity Award, first time given to a poet.

Jay Jii   Poetic thespian. Writer. Composer. Artist. Classical guitarist. Bohemian. Adventurer. Romantic. Like that…

Ryan Jones began writing at an early age. Ryan's topics of interest include nature, human and natural history, mythology, and personal and collective experience. Ryan holds a bachelor's degree in English with a master's degree in childhood education, and works with children by profession.

Evelyn Kandel has been busy writing. She is the author of *Shore Lines, Between Stillness and Motion, Tracing My Shadow,* and *30 Poems 30 Days.* She teaches an adult poetry class, and as one of The Three Poets, gives programs about poetry in local libraries.

Annie Karpenstein is a 2nd generation Holocaust survivor; she is writing a memoir about her life which includes a history of her parents' experiences during the Holocaust. Publications include *Toward Forgiveness, NCPL Review I* and *II, PPA Literary Review #17* and *#18, Sounds of Solace,* and *Bards Annual 2014.*

Nella Khanis is a visual artist, originally from Russia. Experience of both American and Russian cultures brings a special quality to her artistic vision. She feels that she has a Russian accent in speech and in art.

Lois Kipnis is a creative arts consultant. She is the author of *Without a Script: A Caregiver's Journey;* her publications include a one-act play and three educational books. She has a story in *Chicken Soup for the Soul: The Power of Forgiveness,* and her poem "Kaleidoscope" was awarded 2nd prize in an international poetry contest.

Bill Kirsten claims he isn't a poet, writes under stress when his wife, Joan Marg-Kirsten asks him to. However, one of his first poems was selected to be read at a 9-11 memorial, and the next poem he wrote was selected to be included in the *13 Days of Halloween* anthology.

Denise Kolanovic is a poet, teacher and author of *Asphalt Sounds*. She is active in poetry organizations such as Bards Initiative, New York Poetry Forum, and others, and is currently president of All Cities Branch of National League of American Pen Women.

Varteny Koulian grew up in Lebanon during the civil war. She is a graphic artist and lives in Huntington with her husband and English Springer Spaniel.

Mindy Kronenberg's poetry has appeared in print and online across the globe and featured in art installations in the US and Europe. She teaches writing and literature at SUNY Empire State, for Poets & Writers, and BOCES. She publishes *Book/Mark Quarterly Review*, edits *Oberon* Poetry journal, and is on the board of Inspiration Plus.

Born in Brooklyn, **Tonia Leon** has been writing poetry since she was a child. Her poetry reflects her many loves including music, Mexico, trees, ecology, gardening, social justice. She has published poetry and prose in English and Spanish in the USA and abroad.

Faith Lieberman is a poet, sculptor, poetry curato/editor with many degrees. She is the founder/director of Teenspeak Inc and created "Poetry for the HART" produced yearly with the Town of

Huntington; she served 2 terms as Literature panelist NYSCA Trustee; Walt Whitman Birthplace Board Member.

Paul Lojeski was born and raised in Lakewood, Ohio. He attended Oberlin College. His poetry has appeared online and in print. He lives in Port Jefferson, NY.

Chatham Lovette is a LI-based poet/ performer transplanted from the Virginia forests. She is a graduate student and teacher working on her PhD in Philosophy and Feminist Theory at Stony Brook Univ. She performs with the Muse Collective, and tours LI's public libraries for free desks on which to write.

Ed Luhrs started his craft years ago and remains an active participant at events on L and in NYC. His interests, reflected in his writing and performance, include theatrical monologue, humor, dialect, folklore, ancient history, as well as orchestral, jazz, and traditional folk music.

Maria Manobianco is the author of the poetry collections *Between Ashes and Flame, The Pondering Self* and her first young adult fable, *The Golden Orb. She* has a BS in Art Ed from NYU and a MA in Studio Art from Adelphi Univ.

Joan Marg-Kirsten's favorite activity growing up was sitting in a chair next to the window, reading. Now she is a poet and short story writer with many publishing credits, and her husband, friends, and grandchildren write poetry along with her.

Cristina Marie resides in Huntington, LI, where she lives with her three rowdy boys and her doting husband. She is a graduate from

Columbia Teacher's College and works with young children. She has never written professionally and this is her first submission.

Michael McCarthy is a native Long Islander, residing in Port Jefferson with his wife Toni Ann. He teaches theology at the Mary Louis Academy in Jamaica, Queens. He is a lifetime explorer of the sacred and the author of *The Ways of Grace*. goldfinchpublishing.com/ authors/michael-mccarthy.

Brendan McEntee grew up in Queens, NY and acquired his MA in English Literature from Hofstra University. A founding member and editor of *The Triggerfish Critical Review*, his work has appeared in *The Lucid Stone, nowculture, Zygote in My Coffee*, and *madswirl*. He has been anthologized in *Tipping the Sacred Cow*, and *Vintage*.

Gene McParland (North Babylon, NY) is a graduate from Queens College, with several graduate degrees from other institutions. He is the author of *Baby Boomer Ramblings*, a collection of essays and poetry. Gene also performs in Community Theater, mostly home grown original works; and has written several plays.

Florence Mondry leads workshops for OLLI at Stony Brook University. Her poems have been published in *Oberon, Voices Israel, Suffolk County Poetry Review* and other anthologies. She is a retired English teacher and a grandmother of 8. She lives in Setauket.

Marsha Nelson is a playwright, a poet, and a dancer; she received the Ryerson Polytechnic Award, and is a graduate of Hofstra University where she received her BA in Creative Studies; she owns and operates a mobile dog grooming service.

Brendan Noble is an actor/musician/poet here on Long Island. This marks his fourth year in a row getting published in the Bards Annual and is very excited to be able to share some of his work with you.

George H. Northrup is President (2006-) of the Fresh Meadows Poets in Queens, NY; a Board Member of the Nassau County Poet Laureate Society; former President of the NYS Psychological Association, and served on the Council of Representatives that governs the American Psychological Association.

Tammy Nuzzo-Morgan remains.

Michael O'Keefe is a retired 1st Grade Detective from the NYPD. He lives on LI with his family, where he writes a little, and practices the ancient martial arts of lawn and swimming pool maintenance, when he is not coaching football.

Joan Vullo Obergh writes both prose and fiction, and is a 12-time first place poetry award winner. She has been published in numerous magazines, anthologies and journals. Joan is a retired RN and Mental Health Counselor from Seaford, NY.

Tom Oleszczuk has published in various journals and online, hosted readings in Brooklyn, Manhattan, and Sag Harbor. He now lives in Sag Harbor with his wife Heidi and their four cats.

George Pafitis has been writing poetry since 2003 when he retired. He attends poetry workshops at the Great Neck Community Ed Center. Publications include *PPA Literary Review, NCPLS Review,* and *Bards Annual*. He is the author of *Feelings and Words Traveling Together*.

Bruce Pandolfo is a poet, author, rapper and musician based on LI, who tours nationally. He is known by most supporters as "AllOne" the moniker he records, releases and performs his work under. His work is a meticulously dense lyrical attempt to articulate the emotional and intellectual concerns of people.

Gloria Pappalardo is a retired Special Education and English teacher. She has been writing poetry for over 50 years. . She has been published in *PPA Literary Review #18* and #19, *Bards Annual 2014, 2015*, and 2016, and *Freshet*. She is the author of *Grandma's Garden*.

Maria Pigal is a 14-year-old currently attending Farmingdale High School. She enjoys art, writing, and literature and is an editor for Farmingdale High School's literary magazine *Labyrinth*. She usually can be seen staring at a half-finished drawing or poem in frustration, listening to extremely loud foreign music.

Kelly J. Powell is a poet from Long Island...

Pearl Ketover Prilik, poet/writer/psychoanalyst, has had three nonfiction books published, was editor of a psychoanalytic newsletter, two international poetry anthologies and a wide variety of print journals and collections. She lives near enough the water in Lido Beach, NY, along with husband D.J., and Oliver the *humanoid* cat.

Sandra Proto has published two volumes of poetry: a full-length collection *Wrapped Up In Life with Omniscient Eyes,* and a chapbook *Spring's Tepid Breath.* Sandra is also, a crafter (specializing in wooden spoon bottle dolls and mask making); fiction writer, playwright, blogger, and an essayist.

Orel Protopopescu won the *Oberon* prize in 2010 and is the author of a chapbook, *What Remains; Thelonious Mouse,* a picture book; *A Word's a Bird,* her bilingual poetry book for iPad; *A Thousand Peaks* (with Siyu Liu) her book of translations of Chinese poetry. Recent publications include *Light Poetry Magazine* and *Lighten Up Online.*

Barbara Reiher-Meyers is a former board member of LIPC and TNSPS. Barbara has coordinated events for Northport Arts Coalition and Smithtown Arts Council, and conducted poetry workshops for local organizations. Her poetry has been published in print journals and online. Barbara sends weekly emails of local poetry events.

Phil Reinstein, inspired by his late wife Marie, The Insurance Mon is now writing and performing his own poetry songs along with keyboard, accordion and {weak} voice. His politically {in}correct poems have been published in more than a dozen anthologies.

Alphonse Ripandelli's poems draw inspiration from the joy and pain of love. His most recent writings chronicle the interaction and consequences in a relationship that could not flourish.

Jillian Roath earned her BA in Creative Writing from Dowling College. She is an active member of Fanfiction.net and is working on her collection of short stories entitled *13 Dark Tales.* She was one of the founding editors of *Conspiracy*, a genre fiction magazine at Dowling College. She is a certified paralegal and sits on the board for the Bards Initiative.

Rita B. Rose is a multimedia artist who has always had a special love for the Literary Arts. She has gained recognition amongst poetry groups in NY and abroad. She has performed her works for colleges, organizations and social programs. She is presently compiling her poetry into a collection for publication.

Marc Rosen after repeated tests, has been determined to be Chaotic Neutral in personal alignment, and Poetic Neutral in literary alignment. He is Treasurer for The Bards Initiative since its inception. Publications include *Monster of Fifty-Nine Moons and Other Poems*, *Retail Woes*, every *Bards Annual* to date, *The Spoon Knife Anthology*, and scattered e-zines which have since gone defunct.

Gladys Thompson Roth has been teaching a memoir writing class for 15 years to women from Womanspace, an organization originating with the women's movement. She is a prose writer, who started writing poetry as a result of Taproot. Recently, she joined Evelyn Kandel's class in poetry writing.

Miriam Rothermel is the daughter of Narges Rothermel.

Narges Rothermel is a retired nurse. She is the author of *Wild Flowers and Rays and Shadows*. Her poems are published in *PPA Literary Review, Bards Annuals*, and many other anthologies. She has received 1st place award from: Newsday's 2016 Garden Poetry Contest, PPA Haiku Contest, and Princess Ronkonkoma Productions.

Ian Rowan was born in Scotland June 1953. He immigrated to USA in 1982. He never enjoyed reading or writing but found out after the loss of a very dear friend that poetry allowed him to express feelings that he could not speak openly about. Now he enjoys putting feelings into verse and sharing them with friends.

Dorothy Rowlinson was born in Babylon Long Island and is an artist and poet. She spends her winters in Florida and is an active member of the North Port poetry workshop, and the Live Poets on Long Island. She has been published in journals, newspapers and anthologies. Her book "Along the Way" is online at Barnes and Noble, Books a Million; she illustrated it with her art.

Judith Karish Rycar is a retired teacher of English and creative writing. She enjoys writing poetry and has been published in *Moebius Magazine.* Her interests include reading, needlework, and travel.

Dana Sausa is from Long Island. Although she has no home. She lives wherever she roams. Speaks in public forums. She has a voice of her own.

Robert Savino, Suffolk County Poet Laureate 2015-2017, is a native LI poet, born on Whitman's Paumanok and still fishes there, for words. He is a Board Member at both the Walt Whitman Birthplace & the Long Island Poetry & Arts Archival Center. He is the author of *fireballs of an illuminated scarecrow* and *Inside a Turtle Shell.*

Andrea Schiralli helps students with their college application essays; giving them makeovers provides her with "a sense of control in a world full of chaos." A true girly-girl, she's addicted to Hello Kitty, the color pink, and anything that sparkles.

Gregory Schroeder is a teacher, coach, IT analyst, amateur naturalist, amateur historian, daydreamer, observer, participant. He writes for fun and tend to write clean, straightforward poetry and prose in many forms and styles

Karen Schulte is a retired Social Worker and poet. Her work has appeared in a number of publications including *Bards Annual, Suffolk County Poetry Review, Long Island Quarterly, Avocet,* and *Poetica Magazine.* She has won several prizes for her poetry and is a PPA co-host at East Islip Library.

Ron Scott is a member of the Long Island Authors' Group and Long Island Writers' Guild, and Executive VP of the Nassau County Poet Laureate Society. Ron's work has appeared in various anthologies throughout the region. His recent novel, *Twelve Fifteen,* reflects his second hat as a novelist.

N.M Scuri is a writer, editor, teacher, sort-of rugby player, and feline support staff. Her work appears in the anthology Sins of the Past, Thirteen Stories and Paintings, One Bite at a Time, and twice weekly as part of Two Sentence Horrors. She is trying to be the person her Schnauzer thinks she is.

Cathy Silverstein's poems have been published locally in the *Long Island Sounds* anthologies and *PPA Literary Review.* Her restaurant reviews appeared in *Nightlife Magazine,* her only press release was published verbatim by the *New York Times;* she has ghost-written a business memoir for a LI entrepreneur. Cathy lives in Wading River.

Keith A Simmons is a poet/singer/songwriter. He is a staff member of PPA, and Treasurer of the Folk Music Society of Huntington. Professionally, Keith works as a multi-client CFO of LI businesses and serves on the board of Organizational Development Network LI.

Harriet Slaughter has had careers as an actress, singer, dancer, arts administrator, poet and painter. Her book, *ARS POETICA, Sights and Words of a Life,* contains her poetry and paintings. Her poetry has appeared in several anthologies and her artwork has been in juried shows in NY and LI. www.harrietslaughter.weebly.com

Brooklyn born poet **Roger Smith**, earned a BA Cum Laude in English from Molloy College, and writes with a rustic rhetoric and vernacular that speaks to the experiences and struggles of the working middle class American with a family. He is the author of *Laundromats & Lounges* and *Chambers of a Beating Heart.*

Barbara Southard is a writer and visual artist. She currently teaches poetry to children at Whitman Birthplace and serves on the board of LIPC as treasurer and co-editor.

Doreen (Dd.) Spungin is an award-winning poet who hosts for Poets In Nassau and PPA. Her work has been published online, in print journals and anthologies, most recently *Brave Hearts, Grabbing The Apple* and *Syzygy*. Spungin loves love, family, cats, peace and beauty. Truth is good, too.

Gregory Vincent St. Thomasino has poems in the *Bards Annual 2013* and *2015.* His most recent volume of poetry is *The Valise.* He lives in Brooklyn Heights, NY, where in his spare time he writes at his blog, The Postmodern Romantic, and edits the online poetry journal, *Eratio.*

Susan Sternberg is a native New Yorker, an opera singer and supports her writing with a job in marketing. A devoted member of Barbara Novack's South Shore writing group, she began writing last year and completed her first novel this February. "Now" is her first poem.

Ed Stever, Bards Laureate 2015-17, Suffolk County Poet Laureate 2011-13; poet, playwright, actor, director. and author of *Transparency, Propulsion,* and *The Man with Tall Skin.* He compiled and edited *Unleashing Satellite: The Undergrad Poetry Project* and won 1st place in the Village of Great Neck's 5th Annual Poetry Contest.

Kate Dellis Stover has a BA from Columbia Univ in Literature/Writing. She is featured on the CD "Northport Celebrates Jack" reading her prose poem "All Hallows Eve." She wrote the text to *Woman on the Wall*, a collection of photos of graffiti portraying women as goddesses and temptresses.

Jose Talavera was born in NY and is the first in his family to be born and raised in the US. While always interested in the fields of math, science and aviation, and currently studying to be a professional pilot, he was president of Dowling's poetry club for a year. Recently earned his MBA, he remains active in poetry.

Gayl Teller, Nassau County Poet Laureate (2009-11) and Walt Whitman Birthplace 2016 Poet of the Year, author of 6 poetry collections, most recently, *Hidden in Plainview,* and editor of the poetry anthology *Toward Forgiveness*. An award-winning poet, she directs the Mid-Island Y Poetry Series and teaches at Hofstra U.

Maria E. Torres is the author of the poetry book *Secret Thoughts.* She is currently working on publishing a second book. She began writing as a teenager in high school and hopes to inspire other young writers in pursuit of their dreams and love of writing.

J R Turek, Bards Laureate 2013-15, Bards Associate Editor, is 19 years as Moderator of the Farmingdale Creative Writing Group, twice Pushcart nominee, author of *Imagistics, They Come And They Go,* and the forthcoming *A is for Almost Anything.* Poet, editor, workshop leader, host for PPA, and poem-a-dayer, J R, the Purple Poet, lives on LI where she collects dogs, shoes, and poems. msjevus@optonline.net

Don Uhrie is a high school English and Creative Writing teacher, as well as an avid writer. Don has published a poetry anthology, *Whispers from Within.* He hopes to inspire young people to pursue their own goals and to realize the importance and power of language.

Pramila Venkateswaran, Suffolk County Poet Laureate (2013-15) is the author of *Thirtha, Behind Dark Waters, Draw Me Inmost, Trace, Thirteen Days to Let Go,* and *Slow Ripening.* She is an award-winning poet who teaches English and Women's Studies at Nassau Community College.

James P. Wagner (Ishwa) first walked into a Long Island poetry reading at age 17 and hasn't looked back since. At Dowling College he earned his BA and his MALS and has frequently been back to guest lecture. While there, he was heavily involved in their Spoken

Word poetry club. Also while at Dowling, James founded (by accident) Local Gems Press which has since become the unofficial publisher of Long Island poetry—handling yearly publications such as Bards Annual, The Nassau County Poet Laureate Society Review, The Suffolk County Poetry Review, Freshet for Fresh Meadow Poets (Queens) and recently published the Long Island Quarterly 25th Anniversary edition. He is one of the editors of the Perspectives series—poetry concerning autism and other disabilities which went on to become best-sellers. His performance poetry takes some help from his time in musical theater. His latest book "Ten Year Reunion" is available from Local Gems Press.

Margarette Wahl is a teacher's aide in Special Ed for 14 years. She is a PPA co-host at Bellmore Bean Café, an NCPLS Advisory Board member, and Bard's Initiative nicknames her *Bard's Groupie*. She is the author of *Educating By Heart.* She took 1st place in the 2016 NaPoWriMo Chapbook contest held by Local Gems Press.

Herb Wahlsteen earned a BA in English from CA St Univ Fullerton and an MA in English from Columbia U. Publications include *Long Island Quarterly, Great South Bay Magazine, The Lyric, Paumanok Interwoven, Suffolk County Poetry Review, Bards Annual, Form Quarterly, 13 Days of Halloween,* and *String Poet.*

Virginia Walker of Shelter Island is the author (along with Michael Walsh) of *Neuron Mirror*, sales support pancreatic cancer research. She teaches literature courses at Dowling College and Suffolk County Community College. Publications include *Nassau Review, Minetta Review, Light of City and Sea, Touched by Eros, and Bards Annual.*

George Wallace is first poet laureate of Suffolk County, author of 30 chapbooks of poetry and writer in residence at the Walt Whitman Birthplace. Editor of *Poetrybay, Long Island Quarterly* and co-editor of *Great Weather for Media*, he teaches writing at Westchester Community College and Pace University in Manhattan.

Jeffrey Watkins has been a published student of poetic verse since the late 60s on down to the present day and time. He feels his best works are works that exult the virtues of love and human reactions to love's undeniable place in the lives of all…

Marq Wells was first published in 1981 in *Zephyr* magazine. Marq has also been published in *Bards Annual 2011, 2012* as well as North Sea Poetry Scene's *2008, 2009* Editions of *LI\. Sounds Anthology.* Marq serves as IT Tech, event host, and photographer for the Poetry Place since 2009.

Jennifer Marie Vento-West is an English teacher at Legacy High School on Roosevelt Island, NY. She began writing poetry in high school and has been published in several poetry anthologies.

Maxwell Corydon Wheat Jr. **(1927-2016)** a Marine, poet, teacher, activist, naturalist, journalist, editor, a birder, and the 1st Nassau County Poet Laureate (2007-2009); an award-winning teacher of English, for Taproots, for PIER at Hofstra, presented programs on the Hempstead Plains, Adult Ed, at Cedarmere, at Freeport Library, at Theodore Roosevelt Nature Center Jones Beach, a role model to live life with poetry every day. *Rest In Peace, Max.*

Jack Zaffos has been creating poetry since he was 18. Since retirement in 2008 he has increased focus on his writing. Through classes and workshops, Jack is working on refining his work. He is retired from the NYS Office of Mental Health as a Therapeutic Recreation Specialist and an Intensive Case Manager.

Lewis Zimmerman is a Science teacher at Forest Hills High School in Queens, NY. He and his wife Joyce have two daughters, a granddaughter and a grandson. Lewis enjoys poetry, music, reading, travel, comedy, and photography.

Take a Look at These Other Exciting Poetry Publications!

Suffolk County Poetry Review

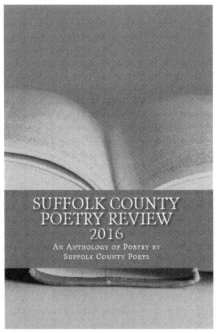

Over 50 Suffolk County Long Island Poets come together to make this volume of poetry in the first volume of the first Suffolk County specific anthology in recent years.

Edited by two Suffolk County Poet Laureates this volume is a true testiment to the poetic talent of Suffolk County.

Available on Amazon!
Published by Local Gems Press

Nassau County Poet Laureate Society Review

Nassau County
Poet Laureate Society Review

Volume III

Featuring the Nassau County Poet Laureate Society contest winners as well as poets from all over Long Island. This thick volume is a pure gem of local quality poetry. Editd by the Nassau County Poet Laureate Society.

Published by
Local Gems Press

Get yours at:
nassaucountypoetlaureatesociety.com

Fresh Meadow Poets Presents
FRESHET

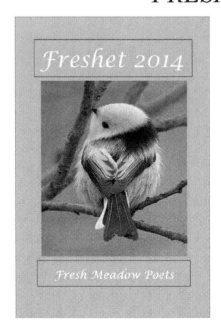

For over two decades the queens poetry group known as the *Fresh Meadow Poets* have been putting out publications.

Take a look at this amazing work of their latest volume and anticipate the next one coming soon. Freset takes submissions by invite only. For more information take a look at their website.

Published by Local Gems Press

http://freshmeadowspoets.org

25 Years of
Long Island Quarterly!

A long time staple of Long Island Poetry, Long Island Quarterly cemebrated it's 25th anniversary.

Long Island Quarterly (LIQ) was founded by George Wallace in 1990. Over the years an estimated 1500 poems by 600 individual poets have been introduced to the world through the publication, ranging from poets with national reputations to those seeing their work in print for the first time.

Published by Local Gems Press!

Available on Amazon!

NoVA Bards 2015!
An Anthology of Northern Virgnia Poetry

A collection of poetry from Northern Virginia poets.

Organized and edited by Bards Initiative VP Nick Hale.

NoVA Bards is the product of many workshops and readings conducted by the Bards Initiative's Northern Virginia Chapter.

NoVa Bards is the "Bards Annual" of Northern Virginia, take a look at what our brother/sister poets are doing!

Published by Local Gems Press
Available on Amazon!

Ten Year Reunion
Poetry of Then and Now...

The latest poetry collection by publisher and Bards Initiative president James P. Wagner (Ishwa)

Ten Year Reunion explores the differences a decade can make, as James looks back to his high school years, remembering growing up in Northport. His 10 year high school reunion brought back a rush of nostalgia that compelled him to write. This book was the result.

Published by Local Gems Press
Available on Amazon!

Editing, Proofreading, Typing

Poet, Teacher, Workshop Leader

Judy (J R) Turek

msjevus@optonline.net

516-481-1131 home

516-644-3458 cell

A multi-purpose poetry project, The Bards Initiative is dedicated to connecting poetry communities, while promoting the writing and performance of poetry. The Initiative provides avenues for poets to share their work and encourages the use of poetry for social change.

In addition, the Initiative aims to make use of modern technologies to help spread poetry and encourage and inspire poetry, particularly in the younger generations. It is the core belief of the Bards Initiative that poetry is the voice of the people and can be used to help create a sense of sharing and community.

www.bardsinitiative.weebly.com

www.bardsinitiative.com

Local Gems Poetry Press is a small Long Island based poetry press dedicated to spreading poetry through performance and the written word. Local Gems believes that poetry is the voice of the people, and as the sister organization of the Bards Initiative, believes that poetry can be used to make a difference.

Local Gems is the sister-organization of the Bards Initiative.

www.localgemspoetrypress.com

Made in the USA
Charleston, SC
14 July 2016